MARVELLOUS MARVIN

MARVELLOUS MARVIN

The Life, Football and Faith of a Soca Warrior

Marvin Andrews
with Tom Brown

MAINSTREAM
PUBLISHING

EDINBURGH AND LONDON

Copyright © Marvin Andrews and Tom Brown, 2007
All rights reserved
The moral rights of the authors have been asserted

First published in Great Britain in 2007 by
MAINSTREAM PUBLISHING COMPANY
(EDINBURGH) LTD
7 Albany Street
Edinburgh EH1 3UG

ISBN 9781845962784

No part of this book may be reproduced or transmitted in any form or by any other means without permission in writing from the publisher, except by a reviewer who wishes to quote brief passages in connection with a review written for insertion in a magazine, newspaper or broadcast

This book is a work of non-fiction based on the life, experiences and recollections of the author. The author has stated to the publishers that the contents of this book are true

A catalogue record for this book is available from the British Library

Typeset in New Baskerville and Stone Sans

Printed and bound in Great Britain by
William Clowes Ltd, Beccles, Suffolk

This book is dedicated to the Almighty God,
Lord Jesus Christ and the Holy Spirit, for saving,
healing and keeping me alive

ACKNOWLEDGEMENTS

Special thanks to my late grandmother, Isadora Andrews, who instilled discipline and love to my life, and to Tom Brown for the transcription and the production of this book. My gratitude also goes to our Prime Minister, Rt. Hon. Gordon Brown, for his support and for making this book possible. And of course my minister, Revd Dr Joe Nwokoye, for Godly counsel, direction and leadership.

Marvin Andrews

Thanks to Valerie Maclennan and Revival Radio; Gavin Peacock and BBC1's *Football Focus*; *Great Glasgow Stories* by John Burrowes and *Glasgow's Giants: 100 Years of the Old Firm* by Dr Bill Murray (both published by Mainstream).

Tom Brown

CONTENTS

Foreword		13
Preface		17
Chapter One:	My Island in the Sun	19
Chapter Two:	New Club, New Life, New Faith	35
Chapter Three:	Livi Lion	49
Chapter Four:	The Rangers Miracle	83
Chapter Five:	Soca Warrior	119
Chapter Six:	Playing the Beautiful Game	139
Chapter Seven:	Kick out the Racists	149
Chapter Eight:	God's XI	163
Chapter Nine:	I'm a Believer	171
Chapter Ten:	The Rover Returns	197
Chapter Eleven:	God is my Agent	205

FOREWORD

The story of Marvin Andrews is one that needs to be told. It is about courage, endurance and commitment to a cause. It is a story that will inspire thousands who read it.

And it is, literally, a story of rags to riches. For Marvin, the rags were all too real – playing football in his bare feet – and the riches don't matter as much as his real aim in life: helping people in distress.

The captain of Trinidad and Tobago (T&T), a Rangers star, a trophy and championship winner, a celebrity in his own right, Marvin could be excused for enjoying the adulation of the crowds and his many fans. But Marvin is a unique individual, interested much less in fame and fortune than in helping those in need.

I do not share or necessarily agree with all of his fundamental beliefs but I respect the work he does in trying to help those who are disadvantaged and admire the leadership he is showing to the younger generation.

He is a young man who cares deeply about people – and his real ambition is to help young people off drugs, out of antisocial behaviour and into a more fruitful life. His desire to help unfortunate young people reflects the impoverished and troubled background from which he emerged with difficulty but in the end triumphantly.

Born on 22 December 1975 in Trinidad and Tobago, Marvin grew up with little. He was brought up by his grandmother. His family could not afford football boots. And his skills were first noticed playing barefoot football.

Marvin played for San Juan Jabloteh and Carib FC of Trinidad. But his schoolteacher and then his first employer – a brewery manager – decided he should have a chance. His teacher found him boots and his employer paid his fare as he shipped him off to chilly Scotland from the heat of Trinidad for trials with Scottish clubs.

The rest is football history: a trial with Motherwell, then a contract with Raith Rovers, sold in 2000, in a deal done over his head – and to the disgust of the Raith Rovers fans – to Livingston, before arriving at Ibrox and becoming a never-to-be-forgotten Rangers legend.

Having made his international debut in 1996, he is currently about to notch up a record of 100 appearances for T&T.

When he made his decision to return to Raith Rovers – and I had the privilege of discussing it with him – it was not just because he wanted to play for Raith but because he knew that in Kirkcaldy, the town he loves, he could do something important to help young people in need.

When I first talked to Marvin, I was astounded by his personal commitment to do good in the community. He travelled hundreds of miles, addressing meetings and telling people about his personal religious faith. Now a minister of his church, he wanted to tell young people on drugs or alcohol that there was hope for them and a brighter future free of drugs and drink. He wanted to run sports leagues that would take young people off

QUOTES FROM FELLOW FOOTBALL PROFESSIONALS

Dwight Yorke (T&T and Premiership): Marvin is a total professional who takes his job very seriously.

Barry Ferguson (captain of Rangers and Scotland): You just have to look at the big man. He's so happy. I think a lot of people should take a leaf out of his book.

Russell Latapy (T&T and SPL): He's a bit of a comedian at times, but us Trinidadians in general are God-fearing people. We do believe and we try to live the right way. That is Marvin's way.

Jim Leishman (Livingston and Dunfermline manager): Marvin believes everyone can be better with God, and I respect him for that. He has certainly proved the doubting Thomases wrong. He is a fantastic team player and one of the best in British football in the air.

Alex McLeish (Rangers and Scotland manager): He is a man of phenomenal faith. We admire him as a person – he's just a terrific human being. He's certainly not shy! He's a gregarious, big lad, always has a big smile and his own style of banter in the dressing-room.

Leo Beenhakker (T&T national coach): He's as safe as the Bank of England.

Ruskin Mark (sports broadcaster): I remember watching Marvin play as a young guy in the local leagues back at home. He is the same Marvin Andrews and has never changed. He is one of the great ambassadors for the game of football, and he continues to amaze me.

With God, nothing is impossible

FOREWORD

the streets – so now the first footballers' trust is being formed: the Marvin Andrews Development Trust.

It is Marvin's personality that has made this possible. The 6 ft 2 Marvin is a gentle giant admired throughout the whole community.

Marvin is doing all this having won most of the Scottish game's major honours: a Scottish League Cup victory with Livingston in 2004, the Scottish Premier League (SPL) championship with Rangers in 2004–05 and the Rangers players' Player of the Year award in 2005.

Modest, unassuming but determined and principled, Marvin enthuses all around him. His religious faith shines through.

His is a story that is yet to be completed, but his first 30 years have made history from the Caribbean to Europe and the stage of world football. He will continue to make history for years to come.

Rt. Hon. Gordon Brown, Member of Parliament for Kirkcaldy and Cowdenbeath

PREFACE

Imagine a barefoot boy, big for his age, kicking a ball on a hot, dusty road under the scorching West Indian sun. A boy with one pair of trainers, one pair of trousers and one T-shirt to his name, playing street football for the sheer joy of the game. A boy whose friends went to the headmaster and begged him, 'Buy Marvin some football boots. He will be the star of our school team.'

Twenty years later, that boy has grown (and then some!) as a man and as a footballer. He has crossed the ocean and reached the highest level in the game, played for a world-famous club, helped to win trophies and championships, matched himself against the best in Europe, and captained his country all the way to the World Cup finals.

He has also become a preacher and pastor. God and the great game of football have done all that for me, Marvin Andrews.

Football took me from my tropical-island home to a land where I knew no one and found new friends and a new family. I joined great clubs and rose to the heights with them. And I shared in the dramas and disappointments that make the headlines.

Above all, I played with pride in my country's colours

and realised the dream I had held since boyhood: to take them to the greatest tournament on the globe.

And, through football, I hope I have given something back. To me, the amazing thing of all has been that the game led me to a new faith and showed me how to promote that faith by playing it.

I have worn the colours of different teams, but under each has been a shirt that proclaims the truth: 'With God Nothing Is Impossible'.

With God, nothing is impossible.

Chapter One

MY ISLAND IN THE SUN

Trinidad is all about the enjoyment of life. Growing up on the island, I always felt part of a close, warm and loving country. To me, it still seems almost like paradise – a tropical island, with long, white beaches and coconut trees, where the days are hot and sunny and the nights are colourful and lively. No wonder the attitude is laid-back and the people seem happy and jolly.

So why leave it? The idea appalled me at first. I had a good job working in a brewery and playing football part-time, and that was all I wanted in life. But God wanted me out of Trinidad and Tobago at that particular time. I had become a man. I had to leave to develop my career and my life – and, at the age of 21, football had become my future.

As a boy, I had played football barefooted, and I lost many a toenail kicking stones or stubbing my feet against concrete. I'd tried using flip-flops in place of trainers or shoes, but they were no good for running or kicking as they just kept falling off. Because we loved the sport so much and played for sheer enjoyment, though, it was no hardship to play barefoot in these five-a-side 'sweat' games.

I would play in a quarry with gravel and rubble

underfoot, but it wouldn't hurt me because the soles of my feet got so tough they were just like the soles on a pair of trainers. If I burst a toe, I would just wrap it up in a piece of cloth and get back into the game.

From as early as I can remember, I lived with my grandmother in a district called Mount Lambert. It wasn't exactly a very playful childhood, because she was extremely strict and kept a very close eye on me. She made sure I said my prayers first thing in the morning and last thing at night and always organised for me to go to church every Sunday, whether I liked it or not.

I don't really know why I wasn't with my mother, but I believe she was into a spiritual cult, and I've been told she tried to offer me up as a young boy to whatever life that cult lived. My dad took me away and put me with my grandmother, who would pray for me to be delivered from all that. I can never forget being in my grandmother's house with my mother standing outside at the gate screaming at the top of her voice, 'Give me my son, give me my son!' My younger brother would spend more time with my mum, but even to this day I don't know the full story.

My grandmother was a very strong woman – not in the sense of bullying or using force on us, but in her determination to bring us up the right way. She was very strict on the principles of living a right life – simple things like being polite, saying 'good morning' and 'good day' to people, respecting your elders. Most of all, she taught me to pray, always to thank God first thing in the morning for the breath of life he has given you and last thing at night for getting you through the day, for keeping you safe and giving you the new day ahead.

Ironically – in view of how I ended up playing for

Rangers in Old Firm games in Glasgow, with their religious background – I started out in the Roman Catholic Church. The largest religious groups on the island are Roman Catholics and Hindus, but substantial Anglican, Presbyterian, Muslim, Methodist, Spiritual Baptist, Orisha and independent fundamentalist/ evangelical Christian groups also exist.

There was a big Catholic church right next to the school in Mount Lambert. My grandmother went to that church, but I came to realise that she was actually a Baptist; she just wanted to get my brother and myself into the presence of God, so she sent us to the church that was within walking distance of our home.

The Catholic Church seemed more understanding and attractive to children than other faiths on the island; their Sunday schools were second to none and they made you want to come to church. I took First Communion and was confirmed as a Catholic, and I am happy that was the foundation for my faith. Later, I went to the Baptists, who have a strong belief in God but do things differently. If anyone had mentioned doctrine to me at that age, I would just have been lost. I had not studied the Bible and didn't know the Scripture in the way I do now, but the Church taught me there was somebody greater than me.

Later on, I realised certain things and saw some bad things and stopped going to church after my grandmother passed away, when I was 13 years old. Even after that, though, I never stopped praying, reading my Bible and trying to be good in my dealings with people. My faith comes from inside me, and I have worked out my own personal beliefs, but at that time I didn't know the true power of faith.

I had been under my grandmother's control, and I'd had to obey her rules as long as I lived in her house. I am not perfect, and I have made lots of mistakes, but I would never think of stealing anybody's stuff, and if we saw anything we wanted, we worked hard to get it so that we could say, 'This is mine', and not that I had done something evil to get it. That is why I would pray a lot, first thing in the morning, last thing at night, before I went to games or when I was going to hang out with my mates.

My grandmother's death from breast cancer was traumatic for me and all of my relatives. We had a big house, and my sisters, brothers, aunties, uncles, cousins and I all lived in it at one time or another, with Grandmother as the undisputed head of the household. Big extended families are not unusual in the West Indies, and I have six sisters and three brothers.

My grandmother's maxim was 'Train your children in the right way so that later on they shall not depart from it', and she has children and grandchildren all over the world who still live as she taught them.

When I went to live with my dad in the Petit Bourg district of Trinidad, I had the freedom to go out and play on the street with my friends. That is when I really got to like football. My cousin Shawn David introduced me to the game, and we would play on the road or in any open space with small goals. Most of the guys on the block were bigger than me and easily knocked me over, but I would just pick myself up and keep playing.

Everyone knows the West Indies have achieved great things in cricket, with famous players such as Sir Learie Constantine, Sonny Ramadhin and Brian Lara making wonderful careers and becoming international heroes.

Football came second, but there was always a great longing, almost a national obsession, for T&T to qualify for the World Cup. I believe this was because of the sense of injustice over what happened in 1974 when we played Haiti and four of our five goals were disallowed – make of that what you will! Then, in 1989, we only needed to win 1–0 against the United States to qualify for the 1990 World Cup in Italy, and we lost out to a freak goal.

I was 14 at the time of that game against America, and by then I was football crazy. I remember the whole population of over a million was consumed by it, and everybody was draped in red. The tickets were over-sold, with a reported 50,000 people in what was a 30,000-capacity stadium; the rest of us were watching on TV sets in shop windows.

When we lost 1–0, to a bizarre goal from a 40-yard shot, it was a devastating let-down. Everybody blamed the goalkeeper, but it just seemed it was not to be, and interest in football went from fever pitch to zero. Those who had been great fans started talking negatively and saying we would never qualify for the World Cup. Many switched their interest to cricket.

I tried cricket, but one time, when I was fielding, the wicket-keeper took a fast ball full in the face, and when I saw the blood pouring down, I decided cricket wasn't my game. Nowadays, that seems crazy, in view of the injuries I have had in football, including gashes in my head with blood pouring out so badly that I had to keep changing my shirt . . .

I started playing football in the street with other boys, so when I passed my Common Entrance and went to junior secondary and there was a call for boys to represent the school, it seemed natural for me to put myself forward.

This is a bit later than boys in Britain start taking football seriously – some are even signed up by big clubs by that age – but I still didn't have a clue.

Russell Latapy, another T&T international who went to Portugal and then Hibs, Rangers, Dundee United and Falkirk, started playing earlier than me and was playing representative football in the Under-10s and Under-14s. Russell came from a family with footballing genius, and he will tell you his older brother was a better player than any of us, but he never got the opportunity on the wider stage.

At Mount Hope Secondary School, I was really encouraged to take it more seriously. The school coach wanted me in defence because I was always big for my age, although I really wanted to be a striker and score goals and celebrate. That was when I discovered my heading ability; when the opposing goalkeeper booted the ball really high down the field, I would get under it and head it back 40 or 50 yards. People were saying 'Oh my goodness, what's happening here?' and they would ask if it wasn't hurting my head, but it was just something that came naturally to me.

From then on, every coach started training me to be a defender, but I still had that desire to be a right-winger or a striker. It is part of my game that I will go up at set pieces and try for a goal – and it has worked, because my career strike-rate is a goal for every half-dozen matches or so.

When I moved on to San Juan Senior Comprehensive, I just watched the school team and didn't really want to play for them. I was a shy boy and not very confident, but in my last year my schoolmates kept asking me to try for the team. I worried that I would be coming up against really good players and tough opponents; believe it or not, I was very timid and scared at that time in my life. Finally, I said 'OK, I'll give it a try' and I made the team.

The coach was Miguel Hackett, who groomed me as a defender because he was a defender himself and a T&T international, and he taught me a lot. He also showed how football could change things in the community, because before he arrived it had been a very violent school. When I first went there, it had been top security, and people going into school were checked for knives and other weapons. Through football a lot of things changed, and young people had something to aim for. If they wanted to play for the school, they could not be involved in these things, and they went on to do something with their lives.

The area I grew up in was not a slum or an especially tough neighbourhood, and there was hardly any violent crime, but people had their problems. There were some people who had knives and guns, including a few of my friends, but I would not even hold them or touch them. I was not stupid, and as you get older, you get wiser. There are always those whose idea of a good time is drinking lager and throwing up. But that can never be enjoying life; it is just damaging yourself.

I was lucky to have such a fine coach as Miguel Hackett training me how to defend properly, how to read the game and how to use my heading ability effectively at free-kicks and corners. I scored five goals for the school from corners, and that season we came third in the league and made two major semi-finals. I repeated my final year to keep playing for the school, and it was a fantastic time for me.

When I left school in 1992, it seemed to coincide with the interest in football in Trinidad coming right back up again, and I went into the screening programme for the national Under-18 team. Over 100 players from different schools took part in the trial, but by this time I was training hard, and I was chosen for the final squad for the qualifying stages of the Under-20s World Cup. We didn't make it to the finals, but it was a big step up from being too scared to go for a school trial. My name began to appear in newspapers, and things like being able to watch myself on TV were very new to me.

At the age of 17 I was very, very proud to represent my country – and I have never lost that feeling. I never looked back from there and made every grade at national level up to the present senior level. The only national teams I never made it into were the Under-14s and Under-16s, but that was because I was a late starter in football.

For a small country, with 1.3 million people, Trinidad and Tobago always had good, talented, naturally skilful players who could juggle and dribble the ball and make pinpoint passes. At the side of the street, you could see young players practising, not just the basic things but difficult and different tricks. You had to be a good defender to stop the tricky players. For us, too, it was not a career or a business pursuit – just a leisure sport full of excitement and community spirit, the joy of playing together and showing off our skills in front of big, appreciative crowds, and a sense of competitiveness that came from fierce inter-community rivalry.

My dad, Anthony Andrews, was a very rugged defender, playing as an amateur, but he had no desire to be professional. He was an engineer, and he worked on the docks for a good wage – enough to buy me a pair of new trainers every month, at the rate I was wearing them out – but Trinidad's economy collapsed and he got laid off, so things became very hard.

That was when I knew abject poverty, but we managed to survive. I remember we lived on bread, sausage and Kool-Aid for months, and I had one pair of jeans, one T-shirt and one pair of trainers, although I was growing out of them at a tremendous rate. The only thing I have ever stolen in my life was fruit, such as mangoes, oranges, pears and sugar cane lying on the ground in people's gardens, because we were so hungry. I could never climb coconut trees, but I had a mate who was very good at it, and I would be the catcher!

Dad went to America hoping to make a better life for us, but he had a struggle and was never able to send for us. Aunts and uncles and others would stand over us and say we were no good, our lives would just be kicking a football about with our mates, and we would never amount to anything. That made me study hard to get through entrance exams and get an education – and it also made me more determined to become something in life.

After my grandmother died, there was a huge family row over ownership of her house, which forced us to leave and live with my auntie in a wooden house in San Juan. She was my father's sister, Claudette Roberts, and I thank God for her. Although my brother and I never disrespected her, we gave her a hard time as teenagers, but she was always there for us and made sure we had things to eat. She would threaten to lock us out of the house, but she always opened the door and loved and cared for us so much. She stuck with us when it would have been easier to give up on us, and she taught me the value of family.

That was a transitional time in my life, and it would have been easy to slip into the street life, but I never forgot what my grandmother said about being honest. We thought loads of clothes and things would be arriving from America, but my dad was having such a hard time over there, working himself to the bone to make ends meet for himself and his wife. I decided for myself that I could not be living like that, depending on my dad and what he could provide for me. I didn't reach the United States to see him until I went there with the national team. It made me so happy and proud that I had managed to visit him purely because of my own efforts.

After I left high school, although Dad sent money to make sure we had food on the table, I needed to get a job. I would go and look for people on the high street and made a dollar here and a dollar there, carrying bags and running errands. I dug toilet holes and even ran to buy drink and marijuana for the older men on the corner, because my life at that time was what we called a 'hustle'. Marijuana, along with all narcotic drugs, was declared illegal in Trinidad and Tobago in 1961, but despite this there were millions of cannabis plants in the forest areas, and the police still enforce the 'Weedeater' marijuana-eradication programme; there was recently a protest song about the hardship caused to the farmers who grew it! When I was growing up, it was so common in my neighbourhood that older men sending me out to buy it was like them sending a youngster out to buy a pack of cigarettes or some groceries. I remember my mum and dad smoking it, but I just never had that desire. I saw enough to teach me the evils of drugs and the terrible effects they can have – and that is a lesson that later made me want to do something about young people who are attracted to drink and drugs.

I tried for a semi-professional football team, EC Motown, sponsored by an electrical firm in the construction industry. I played football there part-time and on other days was a labourer, carrying mortar and toting lumber, which really built me up physically. When I got my pay cheque at the end of the week, it felt so good to be making a life for myself on my own.

After a year, after I had represented my country at Under-18 level, one of my mates called me and suggested I come to play for another semi-professional team, Carib FC, who played in the East Zone, this time under the auspices of the company that made Trinidad's lager. I had an interview with Carib Brewery's general manager, Tim Nafziger, who was later to engineer the move that completely changed my life. Little did I know that was my first step on the road to Scotland!

Mr Nafziger was a huge football fan who supported the team to the hilt. He started me in the merchandising office and set me to cleaning the building. This might not sound much, but I really enjoyed it, because I met so many workers and formed relationships with them. I was so keen that I would get up at 3.30 a.m., say my prayers and start work at 4 a.m. to have everything ready for the office workers starting at 8 a.m.

I was also enjoying the football, especially because we won the league. Most of the football team worked on the production line, where more money was to be made, and Colin Murray, the manager of the brewery football team, got me working shifts on the line. At that time, I started to drink the lager. All of us used to drink a lot. When the manager wasn't about, you would help yourself to a beer. I was working on the line, and all these bottles of lovely, cool lager would be going past, so it was natural to reach out and have one on the spot to quench your thirst. They knew we were helping ourselves but just couldn't catch us. We would have been fired if they had. I realised I had to watch that, because it was just too easy, and I couldn't say how many bottles I'd drink in one day. I was still working hard and training hard, though, and life was so enjoyable.

I could have gone on happily with my life in the brewery and local football for years, but one day in 1997, when I was 21, the general manager said, 'I want you out of here. I'm sending you to Scotland!' He bought me the ticket and put me on the plane to this land that was completely strange to me and previously not even on my radar.

It proved to be a crucial time, because a year later that general manager had a disagreement with the owners and left the brewery. He was the main man and made sure the footballers got anything they needed, but the new management were not big football fanatics and things began to get tougher for the team. There was not the same enjoyment in playing for Carib Brewery.

God knows how and why He does these things, but He used this man to buy me a free ticket. At that time, an air ticket from Trinidad to Scotland cost over 7,000 Trinidad dollars – about 700 pounds sterling. I would never have had that kind of money, and I'd never thought in my wildest dreams about playing professional football in another country. My only desire was to get permanent at the brewery, go on playing part-time and winning with a good team, and go on representing my country. I was making good money, saving steadily and helping my aunt. I was becoming a man.

Although it was just a part-time team, the standard of Carib's football was high. The guys were fit, although they were drinking and enjoying life, and we were a very hard team to beat. Others in our league were playing semi-professionally, especially a club called Joe Public, which was probably paying the highest money on the island. They were owned by a very influential man called Jack Warner, who was president of the Trinidad and Tobago FA and a vice-president of FIFA, and he kept trying to sign me, but I would never go. I just wanted to stay with that brewery team, because I had everything any young guy would want.

It actually hurt me a bit to hear Mr Nafziger say he wanted me to go. But he told me that I was not making the most of my ability and I should go out in the world and show the talent that God had given to me. I had to agree it was an opportunity to play professionally and it was time to stop playing just for the fun of it.

But why Scotland? I would later discover that there are great opportunities for Trinidadian and other players from similarly small nations to play in big clubs in Scotland who nonetheless couldn't always afford the most expensive, most high-profile players. I was to be a part of a great tradition of promising Trinidadian footballers making it big in Scotland. But why did my particular destiny lie there – a place I knew virtually nothing about – rather than in my home country or anywhere else? That is a question I'm still trying to figure out the answer to in full! I have come to believe that it was part of a larger plan for me, a plan that led me to a new faith. I can see that, apart from the success on the football field, or maybe because of it, there is a sense of mission about my being here in Scotland.

Almost before I knew it, I had made the transition, and it was almost like landing on another planet! I didn't have the slightest idea in my head where Scotland was; I knew nothing whatsoever about Scotland or Scottish football. On the TV in Trinidad and Tobago, you got either English or Italian football. When the general manager came up with the idea of moving to Scotland, I had to ask him a second time, because it seemed too fantastic.

He had to tell me that Scotland was in the United Kingdom, and that was all I knew about it – apart from people warning me that, as it was early in 1997 and still winter, it would be very cold. This turned out to be something completely new to me; I had never seen snow before in my life.

For about a year, I was very, very lonely and homesick. I had started to become something at home, and to come to Scotland, a white nation where I did not know anybody, was very, very difficult for me.

After 21 years of excitement and fun in my homeland, surrounded by the people I knew, to come to where the lifestyle was dramatically different, people were talking differently (particularly in Fife!) and I could not understand what was being said to me, where the weather (oh, the weather!) and even the trees were different, was all very hard to deal with.

The first person I met was Stevie Archibald, the famous Scottish international forward, who met me at Glasgow airport and took me to a bed and breakfast in Motherwell, where I sat and wondered what I was letting myself in for.

Stevie was manager of Airdrie at the time and was acting on behalf of my agent – the first time I ever had one – and he took me to Fir Park to try out for Motherwell. That alone was a revelation to me, because Fir Park, although far from being the biggest and best stadium in Scotland, was the kind of football venue I had only played in during representative matches for my country. Our club games in Trinidad were played in small grounds which just did not compare with these big Scottish stadiums.

Alex McLeish was Motherwell's manager at that time. I had an enjoyable two-week trial, but he told me he could not use me because he was looking for more experience. I see now that he was right, because I didn't know the Scottish game and it would take me time to adjust. It may seem ironic that, just over six years later, the same Alex McLeish signed me for Glasgow Rangers, but I needed that time to mature, learn my profession and familiarise myself with a different style of playing.

After the disappointment at Motherwell, my agent spoke to Jimmy Nicholl and Alex Smith at Raith Rovers Football Club in Kirkcaldy. I was not a completely unknown quantity to them because Tony Rougier, a fellow T&T international, had also gone straight from another island club and started his outstandingly successful professional career at Raith. I knew that if I could follow Tony's example, I would be all right.

Although they were struggling in the relegation zone of the Premier League, Raith's recent exploits were still fresh in the mind: winning the League Cup by beating Celtic 6–5 on penalties after a 2–2 draw at Ibrox in 1995, going on to win promotion to the SPL, reaching the second round of the UEFA Cup and going out against Bayern Munich.

MARVELLOUS MARVIN

Jimmy Nicholl, who had achieved all that with Raith, agreed to give me a two-week trial. But that was almost a disaster, because I played my first game against Dundee United at Tannadice and it was very . . . very . . . very cold.

I had never felt so cold in all my life. I had never seen white grass before, far less played on it! I was simply standing there frozen and couldn't understand how people could run about in such weather and on such a surface, but the opposition's strikers were just running straight past me, and we lost 4–0. I was later told that Dundee is one of the coldest places in Britain – and I believe it!

Jimmy Nicholl told me he was going to give me one more chance to prove myself before he sent me back. I was a very determined young man, and I wanted to get a contract and succeed as a professional footballer. I knew I had this one chance left to get my career off the ground or go back to Trinidad and Tobago with my tail between my legs. I had a fantastic game that night at Almondvale against Livingston (my future club), and it was even colder than it had been at Dundee. I put everything behind me, the cold weather and all my worries, and just concentrated on beating the opposition. We won 2–0, and Jimmy didn't waste any time or keep me wondering; he came into the dressing-room after the game and told me I was going to be signed on a two-year contract for Raith Rovers. I was now Marvin Andrews, professional footballer – and a whole new life was opening up before me.

Chapter Two

NEW CLUB, NEW LIFE, NEW FAITH

Raith Rovers will always be a very special football club for me because of the start it gave me and for all that it brought into my life. It was at Stark's Park, the Raith Rovers ground, that I realised how important football was to me and what I might achieve if I dedicated myself to becoming a full professional – but there was no way I could have known what else would lie in store in Kirkcaldy.

When Jimmy Nicholl told me he was going to sign me under contract for Raith, I was on a high. Then came the let-down when I was told the next necessity was to leave the UK for three months!

I had to go back to Trinidad and Tobago and work in the brewery until my British work permit came through. I was just waiting and praying and hoping that everything would go well and there would be no hitches, because I could not bear the thought of any barrier between me and professional football.

I could see the game was growing bigger and bigger on a global scale, and I wanted to be part of that. I wanted to test myself at a higher level, live outside my country for the first time and be able to help my family back home. I realised I was becoming a man and had to do something with my life, not least being able to take money out of my pocket and do something to support my folks.

I officially became a Raith Rovers contract player on 1 September 1997 at the age of 21, which is late in life to become a pro footballer. By that age, most players have a few years of professional experience behind them.

Although I had one or two on-and-off mates from the team, it was a very trying and lonely time for me. Again, I got lucky, because I was put into Linda and Harry Duffy's bed and breakfast in Pratt Street, Kirkcaldy, right opposite Stark's Park. I lived with them for four years, during which time they looked after me, taught me about the customs and history of my new country and just provided a home and family support for me.

They virtually adopted me, so that I now call them 'Mum' and 'Dad'. Even when I went to Livingston, I stayed on in Kirkcaldy with them and only left because I had gathered so much stuff that my room was closing in on me. When I told them I had to move, they were devastated.

It was so touching for me, as a black person, to have that first contact with two white people, and they showed me that Scottish people were so lovely and friendly. They never once paid any attention to my colour or judged me because of my race. They saw me as just a human being, and that helped me to adjust and settle down in Scotland more easily than I might have done. Kirkcaldy and its people gave me the perfect introduction to Scotland.

I had a great relationship with each of the Raith players with whom I shared my room over the years at Linda and Harry's. They used to make fun of me because I would be up at 6 a.m. in our shared room to pray while they would still be trying to sleep. When they were watching the TV, I would be reading my Bible. They were not used to it but accepted that it was something I needed to do.

I have a lot to thank those guys for because they helped me to get used to all sorts of things, such as fish and chips and Scottish soup. Soup in Trinidad is a meal in itself, with all sorts of different things in it, like dumplings, so Scotch broth took some getting used to . . .

It was the most exciting time for me, even though I had come to Scotland at the worst time of the year. People who are accustomed to the climate don't realise what an effect a Scottish winter can have on you when you experience it for the first time. My hands were completely numb throughout my first game as a full Raith player, a 1–1 draw against Airdrie. In those early days in Scotland, the cold weather was such a problem for me that I phoned my former coach at Carib FC, Colin Murray, and told him it was getting to me. I even said I was thinking of coming home to Trinidad, but he told me, 'Stick it out.'

Of course, he was right. I just had to learn to tough the climate out, but I did laugh at the description of one sports writer, Jock MacVicar, who wrote that I had good reason to be pleased with my debut because I had done more than a competent job, although, 'In Trinidad, unlike Kirkcaldy, the sun is hot and the population does not walk round in winter with a permanent drip on the end of its nose.'

As I tried to adjust to the Scottish style of playing and the ground conditions, my first five games for Raith went yellow card, yellow, yellow, yellow and yellow, then I got a red! I was extremely keen to succeed and had always been an aggressive player, but I had to adapt to suit the referees.

Jimmy Nicholl said later that he had no idea I would turn out to be such a valuable player. I was pretty raw, and what got me by was fitness, enthusiasm and the fact that I was so aggressive. Trinidadian defenders are made that way: fearless, hard challengers and trained to win in the air. That is why Scotland was such a good move for me, because that style fitted in perfectly with the Scottish game.

In those early matches, I realised the Scottish game was much faster and the pace had to be maintained for the entire 90 minutes, but I was confident I could get used to it. Later, I picked up quite a few knocks and bangs, and in one game against Hibs I ended up with one eye closed and the other stitched up by the club doctor.

I am the first to admit that I can be clumsy, and my type of play, especially going for balls in the air, is bound to lead to clashes – but it was also the effect of adapting to the Scottish game, which is all about commitment and giving no quarter.

Raith seemed a healthy enough club to join, with a playing staff of more than 30 and the covered, all-seater stadium that was needed to play in the Premier League. I only discovered later the financial state that is only too typical of so many Scottish clubs: Raith had amassed a huge overdraft to pay for it and were having to sell off their best players to keep afloat.

Without the money Raith got in transfer fees, they could not have supported full-time football at that time, and we got used to losing our best players. That was one reason why players like me were good signings – we were experienced internationals in our home countries but unknown in Scotland, so we cost nothing. That is not a complaint on my part, because it worked to my advantage and gave me a great opportunity.

In my first season with them, I was happy to be part of a reasonably successful side under Jimmy Nicholl, who is a good coach, an outstanding tactician and very well liked. Although players who had been part of Raith's prior success had been transferred, the team stayed in the top three of the First Division in the 1997–98 season. We started with confidence, but we just could not get the all-important away wins and were never really promotion contenders. We ended five points behind Falkirk and ten points behind Dundee, whose new owners were putting money into the Dens Park club and who won promotion to the Premier League.

My second season with Raith was a different story, as the club paid the penalty for its behind-the-scenes problems. That 1998–99 season was just a battle for survival in the First Division, and we managed to stay up . . . just. There was a lot of financial pressure, and it was hard to concentrate while we knew the club was under the threat of bankruptcy. It was a vicious circle, and it meant the fans were not getting anything to shout about, especially when we took a 6–0 hammering at home from St Mirren, which stays in my mind as the worst result I have ever had against me.

Despite that dark background at Stark's Park, I was improving my game and enjoying myself. That was until I pulled my groin and the injury developed into something really serious – an inflammation of my pelvis bone.

What brought on and aggravated the condition was the fact that I was training on heavier grounds than I had been accustomed to. I was working with the injury, feeling good one week, and then I would break down the next. It was getting more and more frustrating for me, and I knew that I couldn't go on like that because I would be of no use to the team. It looked as if I might see the season out playing through the pain, but I would then have to go back to Trinidad, because no manager wants a player who keeps breaking down.

I was told there was nothing they could do but remove the inflammation by giving me tablets or an operation that involved putting a metal plate in my abdomen. I said I was not prepared to do that, and that is when an amazing thing happened.

My mate Tony Rougier from Trinidad, who had played for Raith and was still living in Kirkcaldy, although he was negotiating a move, said he was going to take me to the church. I had never gone to a church in Scotland before.

Tony introduced me to Pastor Joe Nwokoye, the spiritual leader of the Zion Praise Centre in Kirkcaldy, who also held healing services. It must have been planned, because two weeks later Tony left Raith for Hibs, and if I had not had the injury just at that time, I would not have received healing.

When I told Pastor Joe my problem, he told me that God could heal me. Now, I had always believed in God, but I had no idea of the true purpose and power of belief. As I had nothing to lose, I thought I would give Him a chance.

Pastor Joe showed me different parts of the Bible where Jesus had healed the sick, opened the eyes of the blind and performed his great miracles. We prayed together, and I kept on praying on my own. Meanwhile, I accepted the club's physiotherapy and went on the treatment table, but I was under contract to them for another year and they wanted me to take the surgery. It was a complete surprise for them when I told them the operation would not be necessary, as God would treat me in the right way. They were sure that the metal plate was the only way I could continue my career. Then, one day, I woke up and the pain was gone. I was able to carry on playing without any setbacks. In fact, I went on to win the Raith supporters' Player of the Year award. From that day to this, I have not suffered that pain again.

The doctors were actually speechless, and from that moment I committed myself to Christ. I know it wasn't God who gave me that injury; I believe it was the Devil, who was trying to strike me down. I trusted in God, who overcame everything. Some people say that what happened to me is mind over matter, but I know it is faith over matter. I believe it was God who healed me. It was my first step of faith, discovering that prayer could heal a physical problem.

At the time, unlike later occasions when my faith and my football became intertwined, a big deal wasn't made of it in the press or anywhere else because I was not yet a well-known player. It was simply between me and the club.

I had always prayed a lot when I was a youngster, asking for protection for my family and myself, but after that I became more active, and my life has really revolved around the church. All the lads at the Scottish clubs I have played for know what I stand for and accept me as I am.

Jimmy Nicholl and Alex Smith were fired in my second season, and I will always be grateful to them for the gamble they took on an unknown like me. They gave me the opportunity to prove myself, and it opened the door to a new life for me in so many different ways.

It was obvious to everybody that a new approach had to be tried. John McVeigh and Peter Hetherston took over and things changed almost immediately; we were defending better and everyone was working hard to produce goals. I really believed we could win promotion back into the Premier League. We had a lot of talent and potential in our side, which was proved by the number of players who went on to bigger things, but consistency was our problem.

In December 1999, it was obvious there were still ructions behind the scenes when, despite turning the team round on the park, John McVeigh lost his job. His assistant Peter Hetherston was not happy and took time to consider his position before agreeing to take over.

In the dressing-room, all we could do was show the spirit John McVeigh had created in us, and while the future was still up in the air we played our hearts out for the club and for Peter as caretaker manager, as was shown with a 4–2 win over Inverness Caledonian Thistle that must have helped confirm Peter in the job.

I got a couple of goals early in the season but wanted more. I am always looking for goals when we have free-kicks and corners. We really showed what we could do in a game against Livingston at Almondvale in September 2000. They were top of the table and favourites to go up to the Premier League, but we caused a sensation by beating them 4–0. I scored two. The first one was a typical header and the other was a cool finish from a ricochet when everybody expected me to blast it in – or over. It was only the second time I had ever scored with my foot, and the first was for my national team. We knew then that, despite our disastrous start, we would be there or thereabouts in the shake-out for promotion at the end of the season.

By this time, I was accustomed to the style of play in Scotland. After the laid-back game in Trinidad, I was beginning to appreciate and enjoy the faster approach.

It was a hectic time for me because it was right in the middle of the T&T campaign to qualify for the 2002 World Cup finals in Japan and South Korea – and we were having a great run, unbeaten in the initial qualification stage with 13 goals for and none against.

I was doing well at Raith Rovers at a time when every game was important to the club and points were vital. Yet that was exactly when the national team would send a letter saying 'We need Marvin Andrews', even when it was just a friendly game and nothing important.

Somehow, players with bigger clubs such as Manchester United were given dispensations, but, because Raith Rovers were a smaller club that struggled to have any rights, the national management put the pressure on. These demands had to be taken seriously because there was always the danger of disciplinary action through the international bodies against the club or myself.

It isn't as if they timed the fixtures to create an international week or to take advantage of a Scottish league shutdown, when there were no club fixtures. Any management would be unhappy about losing one of their main players at a time when three points could cost the club promotion.

All I wanted to do was play football, and I was caught in the old 'club or country' dilemma. If I went to T&T and Raith didn't get the result they needed, I was to blame

MARVELLOUS MARVIN

– but there would be a backlash at a higher level if the club couldn't release me.

After the Livi win, Peter Hetherston asked me to put my World Cup qualifier appearances for T&T on hold. He said at the time, 'I'm glad to get Marvin back for two weeks, because we usually see him for a week and then he's flying off again.'

I was committed to winning promotion for Raith as well as reaching the World Cup finals with T&T. The problem was partly solved when T&T won in Canada. I was sent off in the last minute, which meant I was suspended for the game against Mexico.

To tell the truth, I had been tempted to stay behind after the Canada game and see my dad in New York, but I wanted to play for Raith against Celtic in the CIS Cup, so I got a helicopter to the airport to catch the flight back to Scotland.

Another time, after I scored in a World Cup qualifier against Dutch Antilles, I missed my connecting flight and was delayed in Miami. Because it happened to be carnival time at home, I was accused of deliberately missing the plane and then hopping over to Trinidad to live it up – but I do not tell lies. I was kicking my heels in Miami and did some running and went to a gym to keep up my fitness until I could get the first plane back to Britain.

Relations became strained when I had to miss a crucial Fife derby against Dunfermline, just when Raith were contending for promotion. It was the last throw of the dice for Raith, because anything less than a victory would end our chances of overtaking Falkirk and getting into a play-off spot. Peter Hetherston made a personal plea to the T&T boss Ian Porterfield, explaining to him the importance of the Dunfermline game. Ian phoned back to say he had been through all the permutations but he had no one to play in my position. Naturally, the Raith management were not happy and accused T&T of 'double standards', since Tony Rougier, Russell Latapy and Dwight Yorke had all been excused, yet there was no cover for me.

Manager Peter Hetherston said, 'Marvin is a key player for us, and it is my opinion that, had we had him for the whole season, we would have been set for promotion.

'We have always known that Marvin is a Trinidad and Tobago internationalist, but it is the huge number of games he has to play for them which frustrates me.'

At the end of the 1997–98 season, Dundee and Falkirk went up into the SPL and Raith came a close third. I had a fantastic season, scored four or five goals and was made Player of the Year.

After Raith missed out on promotion, they actually announced they would impose a ban on signing foreign players likely to be capped by their country. They said it was not right for the club to have to pay a player when he was away on international duty. The financial director at the time, Colin McGowan, pinned it squarely on me by saying, 'It cost the club thousands of pounds when Marvin Andrews was away with Trinidad and Tobago and we still had to pay his wages. I don't even know where Trinidad and Tobago is, but all I know is that it's a long way from Kirkcaldy.' What I knew was that I had no intention of giving up the honour of representing my country.

As I was going to be out of contract at the age of 24, it was time to consider all my options. Clubs north and south of the border were enquiring about me, and my international teammate Dwight Yorke, who was playing for Manchester United, was giving me advice. With the right club, the right terms and the right feeling, with regard to my spirituality, I would be happy to stay in Scotland, because I had come to love the country and the people, but I also wanted to play against the best players, so a move to the English Premiership could not be ruled out.

I got a lot of stick from the Raith players when Ebbe Skovdahl, then manager of Aberdeen, was said to be offering £100,000 for me. In the dressing-room, they were talking Aberdonian to me, which I found even harder to understand than the Fife dialect! There was also mention about sheep, but I didn't know what all that was about, so I just laughed anyway . . .

I was really enjoying my time at Raith and the good friends I had made in Kirkcaldy and had mixed feelings about whether I should stay or go, but in the end a financial crisis came along and forced change on me – something that was to happen again later in my career. I told the chairman Danny Smith that I still wanted to stay, but he said, 'I would love you to stay, but I don't know if I can pay your wages next month.' It was as plain as that – so I left my first Scottish club in September 2000.

In a multi-player deal, Alex Burns, Stevie Tosh and I were all sold by Raith Rovers to Livingston. To this day, I have no idea what fee was involved for me, but it was said that Raith were 'between the devil and the deep blue sea' and the money for me would reduce the club's debt by around £50,000.

By contrast, Livingston's owner Dominic Keane could afford to pump money into his club, building up a very strong team with big ambitions. Their manager Jim Leishman said he had had his eye on me for some

NEW CLUB, NEW LIFE, NEW FAITH

time, and I suppose my performance in the 4–0 win at Almondvale, in which I scored the two goals against his side, finally made up his mind.

Jim Leishman, who had spoken very persuasively about his vision for Livingston and the part I could play in it, said he knew I would play it straight down the line with him and left it to me. He was so supportive that he came to one of our prayer meetings at the church in Lochgelly and heard an American gospel choir.

Jim said later, 'I was sitting at the back while Marvin was up front with his fellow worshippers, and I thought it was tremendous. What a faith and belief to have.

'Most people will say they believe in God, but it was really humbling to be there. Some people may say it is a false belief, but big Marvin has true belief, and I really admire that.'

Just a few months after that victory for Raith, Alex Burns, Stevie Tosh and I were playing against them in the Livingston strip, and we beat our old club 2–0. One report reminded Raith that they should have known all about the 'awesome power of Marvin Andrews' heading ability', because the first score came from a 40-yard header that caught Rovers' defence unawares; it dropped at the feet of Alex Burns, who flicked it over our former teammate Guido van de Kamp in goal.

That's football for you . . .

Chapter Three

LIVI LION

Livingston Football Club had been in existence for just five years, and I was lucky to join them when they were making soccer history. They were well named the 'Livi Lions' because they feared nobody and were willing to take on – and beat – the biggest clubs in Scotland and Europe.

My transfer may have been forced on me by the financial circumstances at Raith Rovers, but I would not have missed my time at Almondvale because it was exhilarating, exciting and rewarding.

From the other side of the Firth of Forth, I had watched Livingston come from nowhere to become a real force in Scottish football. Formed from what had been Meadowbank Thistle in Edinburgh in 1995, the season before I arrived in Scotland, they relocated to the new town of Livingston in West Lothian.

From their very first season, they took off like a rocket and zoomed up through the divisions. There seemed to be no stopping them as they won the Third Division championship in their first season and within five years had charged up through the Second and First Divisions into the SPL.

When I signed for them on 28 September 2000, it was

made very clear to me by the owner Dominic Keane and manager Jim Leishman that they had big ambitions and I was part of a move to strengthen the team because they were not going to be content spending time in the First Division. They were determined to make Livingston a top-flight club, and they were putting together a team that would challenge the very best.

They were right, too – at the end of the season, the Livi Lions were presented with the First Division trophy at the Caledonian Stadium in Inverness. We had booked our place in the SPL and were ready to take on Rangers and Celtic.

We showed what we could do against SPL opposition when we met Aberdeen on our home ground in the fourth round of the Scottish Cup. There was a feeling that we could use the match to demonstrate our readiness for the SPL and we took the game to them straight from the kick-off.

Aberdeen were a good test of how we would fare in the top division because they were on a solid run, having gone four games in the SPL without conceding a goal. They had also reached both Hampden cup finals the previous season.

The match ended in a goalless draw, but I was disappointed because in the 78th minute I almost put Livi ahead when I went up to meet a cross into the box and my header smacked off the underside of the crossbar.

For the replay at Pittodrie, one pundit dismissed our chances, saying, 'Aberdeen will want to show who are the Premier League side.'

The Monday night game had to be postponed when heavy overnight snow made conditions hazardous. It went ahead two nights later, although the conditions were still horrendous, but by now I was accustomed to the Scottish winter.

Aberdeen, this time with home advantage, started out as if they meant to play us into the ground, but we held out and by half-time were giving as good as we got. In the second half, the Dons began to get frustrated because they could not break us down. Robbie Winters, always a dangerous forward, almost gave them the winner, but I managed to block his shot and turn it out for a corner. When Scott Crabbe popped up to head us in front with eight minutes remaining, what was described as 'Livingston's well-organised rearguard' held on grimly.

Livingston were treated as 'giant-killers', but we saw it differently. To us, it was doing the necessary against a club that would be in the same higher division as us in a few months' time, and we were quite rightly rated 'a Premier League outfit in waiting'.

In the quarter-finals, we had no trouble seeing off Peterhead 3–1, but it was a different story in the semi, when we were drawn to meet Hibs at Hampden Park. We lost 3–0, but it was agreed that we did not deserve such a wide margin of defeat.

The day had started with high hopes, and our fans were celebrating at Almondvale before we even set off along the M8 to Glasgow. But our build-up had been hit by injuries to our two goalkeepers and, as a standby, efforts were made to draft in Russian international Dmitri Kharine on loan from Celtic.

In the event, although he was not fully fit, Ian McCaldon was in goal, but his first touch was to pick the ball out of the net. To be fair, no one could have stopped John O'Neil's thunderous shot from 14 yards.

Midway through the second half, I came within inches

of equalising when my header from a corner took a cruel deflection and just cleared the crossbar. Minutes later, one of those problem balls came back at me – a high awkward return from our goalie's clearance. Ian McCaldon came flying out to get it, and Zitelli took advantage of our hesitation with a clever overhead kick into the empty net. Seven minutes later, it was all over when we lost another goal to a screaming 20-yard shot, and Hibs went on to the final, which they lost 3–0 to Celtic.

However, we had far from disgraced ourselves and could take consolation from the fact that in six years Livi had gone from nothing to the semi-final of the Scottish Cup while preparing to enter the Premier League.

The statistics make winning the 2000–01 First Division championship look easy. We finished seven points clear of second-placed Ayr United, having won twenty-three of our games, drawing six and suffering only six defeats in the season. The fact that 31 goals were scored against us, while we put 72 past our opponents for a goal difference of plus 41 showed how well organised our defence was.

But statistics do not tell the whole story. There were some tough matches, especially against Ayr United, who scored more goals than us, and Inverness Caledonian Thistle, who had an amazing mid-season run but finished fourth. Under Steve Paterson, Inverness had a 14-game unbeaten sequence, including a 7–3 victory over Ayr United, their fellow promotion chasers.

On 28 April 2001, we needed only one point against Inverness to confirm that the championship was ours. When we beat them 3–2 after a hard-fought game, our travelling fans who had made the long journey to Inverness celebrated with a pitch invasion.

In our first month in the SPL, we were the surprise package and I won the Player of the Month award. Everybody expected us to be the whipping boys, but we proved them all wrong. When Rangers and Celtic came to Almondvale, they knew they were in for a good game.

It really stung our pride when we were described in the media as 'johnny-come lateleys' and even 'a pub team'. That did not show us the respect we felt we had earned; but it showed how many people feel about Scottish football – that there is an 'establishment' of about half a dozen teams and the rest are outsiders. They should give credit to teams like Livingston and Inverness Caledonian Thistle (and, now, Gretna) who have built themselves up from nothing and brought something new to the game.

We were not going to be content just with establishing ourselves in the Premier Division. Already, we were ambitious to get up alongside the Old Firm, and I, for one, wanted to see us getting into Europe.

We achieved all that in our first season at the top level, when we came third in the SPL and qualified for Europe. It was a new club in a new stadium in a new town, and there was a feeling of growing together. There was always a good atmosphere and the sense of the local people bonding with their team; I am certain that the football club played an important role in turning a new town into a community.

I believe Livingston set an example that other small clubs can follow. All it takes is a wealthy backer, a board of directors as enthusiastic as the players, a larger-than-life manager, experienced coaches who know what they are doing and a pool of players from around the world who can play as one . . . !

At one time, we had nine different nationalities in our team, including the Togo international Sherif Toure Maman, Italian Simone del Nero, Frenchman Didier Santini, the Spaniards Rubio and Camacho, Canadian Xausa and the Argentinian striker Fernando Pasquinelli. Later there was Theodore Whitmore from Jamaica, a skilful and very tricky midfielder who had given me a lot of trouble when we were on opposing sides in Caribbean matches, and a Brazilian coach, Marcio Maximo Barcellos.

The remarkable things we achieved at Livingston in that first SPL season all became possible because of the unity within our ranks and our positive approach, refusing to be intimidated by the big clubs like Rangers and Celtic.

We showed how a club can set a target, achieve it and then move on to the next, higher, objective. Initially, we had to establish Livingston in the Premier League and avoid dropping straight back down to where we had come from. When we were safe, midway through the season, we set our sights on a top-six finish, and from there it was on to qualifying for Europe.

Winning the SPL Player of the Month award so early in the season was a big thing for me, because it confirmed that I really had arrived. The real test would be playing Rangers and Celtic, and the fixture list threw us in at the deep end. However, even though we were the new boys, we were not overawed; instead, we took the game to them and took a point off both of them.

Against Rangers, I had a good game against Tore Andre Flo. In our 1–1 draw against Martin O'Neill's Celtic, I had to cope with Henrik Larsson – a very special footballer in every respect – and John Hartson, who was a very physical player and out to make his mark in one of his first appearances for the club. It was a big thing for me that I was named the Man of the Match against such quality opposition.

There were complaints that Livingston were 'occasionally over-robust' and 'tackled like dervishes', but these were rough, tough opponents who would intimidate you if they could. To survive, you had to show them you could give as good as you got.

After our first game against Celtic at Almondvale, a Sunday paper commented: 'If John Hartson thought Scottish defences were going to be a soft touch, he will have the bruises and aches to disprove that notion this morning.'

I managed to make my mark at both ends of the field. In the Celtic penalty box, I got my head to a free-kick from Barry Wilson and it went just wide. At the other end, I slipped on the wet turf and Hartson ran past me into the box to pick up a pass by Sylla. I was determined not to give away a goal on half-time and galloped back to make the tackle, whipping the ball off Hartson's toe and away for a corner.

For me, however, the real highlight of the game was when Larsson took a penalty late in the game, which would certainly have given Celtic victory. I could not watch as he walked up to the spot, but I started to pray and I knew God would answer me. Henrik struck it well, but our keeper, Javier Sanchez Broto, managed to deflect the ball over the bar. Mind you, I have to give credit to Broto, who did brilliantly. He seemed to specialise in saving penalty kicks, as we had learnt to our cost the previous season when he was with Airdrie and they beat us in a penalty shoot-out in the final of the Challenge Cup.

Afterwards, a reporter asked me what would have happened if Larsson had also prayed. I just grinned and said, 'God would have answered the person who believes more!'

My post-match remarks about asking for God's help with the penalty made a lot of headlines, such as 'God 1: Henrik 0', 'Marvin's Prayers Answered', 'God Saved Us' and 'Livi's God Squad'. That made me happy because it showed that, playing at that higher level, my testimonies to the power of prayer would get wider attention. To me, it was more proof that, with the Lord, all things happen for a reason.

Suddenly, I was playing in front of capacity home crowds of 10,000. For the first time, I was making big money from my football, but it was important for me not to forget my roots. I was able to do things like send boots and strips to my old club back in Trinidad, to help to give other players the opportunity to make the most of their talents and follow in the footsteps of people like Russell Latapy, Dwight Yorke and myself.

I was getting a lot of credit for my work in Livingston's defence, where I had formed a good partnership with Oscar Rubio, but I wasn't getting the goals as I used to, although I still managed to score when I played for my country. In fact, for a long spell, my last goal at Almondvale was for Raith Rovers against Livi! The chairman, directors and management were all begging me to score, and the manager, Jim Leishman, was urging me to get up there and hit the target, never mind score. He complained to the press, 'Last year, Marvin scored two goals against us. We liked what we saw, so we signed him – and he hasn't been on target since, including in training!' My first goal for the club came in a 5–1 away win against Kilmarnock, who were then used to finishing in the top four of the SPL and getting into Europe – and I made a point of dedicating my goal to Jim and the board of directors!

Despite some high-scoring wins, it seemed as if everyone else in Scottish football thought we were a flash in the pan, and they kept waiting for the Livingston bubble to burst. First, they said we wouldn't win promotion from the First Division, and when we did, they said we were lucky. Even when we demolished a fine side like Aberdeen 6–1 in the CIS Cup, after draws against Rangers and Celtic in the league, some people said it was a fluke. When you are successful, there are too many in football who begrudge you that success, look on the negative side and want you to fail.

Even more important for me was the news I received that on 11 September 2001, the day of the terrorist attack on the World Trade Center, my dad was OK. He worked as a mechanic in that part of New York, and I feared the worst. I spent several frantic hours trying to find out what had happened to him, but I got word that he had been heading out of Manhattan just as the first plane hit the skyscraper block.

Games against Celtic were always bruising encounters, and we were under orders not to let ourselves be shoved around and dominated physically. In one Sunday game, Stilian Petrov and I clashed in the penalty box. Although it was a pure accident, I was penalised, and that gave Henrik Larsson the first of his two goals in the match. There was nothing malicious in our collision, just two big men going for the ball. When I went in for the challenge, I think his face hit my chin. I honestly did not know much about it. I was dazed and bewildered, and when I recovered I could see blood pouring from Stilian's mouth. Afterwards, I was told he'd been given as many as 15 stitches both inside and outside his mouth, and I felt sick. I sent him my best wishes because Celtic were playing the Spanish side Celta Vigo in the UEFA Cup the following week, which was good for Celtic and Scottish football. Luckily, he made that game.

Sometimes even innocent bystanders can get into the firing line – and I was horrified when I was the cause of a ball-boy getting a full-power clearance in the face. Early in a Rangers game, I had to make an interception in a dangerous area; maybe I could have just clipped the ball out, but you don't want the other team to intercept, so I decided to really hammer it into the stand or even over it. I hit the ball with everything I had, but unfortunately it stayed low and hit our ball-boy, 13-year-old Scott Stewart, full in the face. It was appalling to see Scott lying there for maybe five minutes before being carried around the track by the club physio and taken in to be checked in the medical centre. Happily, he was only dazed, and when we met up later, he said I was still one of his favourite players – but for the next game the club made him the mascot and kept him out of the line of fire!

That incident was upsetting enough, but that Rangers game – in front of a capacity 10,000 crowd and the Sky TV cameras at Almondvale – just got worse for me. In the 65th minute, Tore Andre Flo was racing in on our goal and I went in, tackling him in the penalty box. I definitely got the ball, and Flo went over my foot, but Oscar Rubio also came in and their feet may have tangled. Referee John Underhill deemed I had fouled Flo, gave me a red card and awarded Rangers a penalty, after which they won 2–0. I am not the kind of player who gets sent off, but the referee made his decision and I had to put up with it. With God, everything happens for a reason, and there must have been one for what happened to me – but I still can't see what it was . . .

It was a big disappointment because if we had managed to win that game, we would have been only one point behind Rangers at the top of the SPL. We gave it everything we had, and as we came off the field, Jim Leishman and his assistants shook our hands in recognition of the fact that we had worked so hard.

It was that hard work and commitment which took us to third place in the SPL in that 2001–02 season. Celtic ran away with the championship with an astonishing 103 points; Rangers were runners-up on 85 points (although they beat Celtic in the Scottish Cup final and also won the CIS Cup as consolation); and we came third on 58 points, beating Aberdeen to the UEFA Cup place by three points. It was another amazing chapter in the Livingston success story – with more drama still to come, on and off the field!

Livingston's first-ever European tie was a trip to Liechtenstein to take on FC Vaduz in the qualifying round of the UEFA Cup – and I missed it because of chickenpox. It was a real disappointment because I had trained hard for that important game in the club's history and was in the team hotel when it was diagnosed. We drew 1–1 in the first leg in Liechtenstein, and luck was on our side in the second leg at Almondvale because we hung on to a 0–0 draw which put us through on the single away goal. It was a narrow escape. Vaduz won a late corner in the dying seconds, the ball was sent into our box and Marius Zarn shot into the back of our net. However, the referee blew the whistle for full-time before the ball crossed over the line and declared it a no goal because the game was finished.

Our next opponents, in the first round proper, were Sturm Graz, who had made themselves a force to be reckoned with in the Austrian Bundesliga. In recent seasons, they had swept the board in their league, cup and super-cup and were regulars in the Champions League, sensationally winning their 1999–2000 group against Galatasaray, Rangers and Monaco.

We still thought we were in with a chance for the match in the Arnold Schwarzenegger Stadium (a name which made us smile – no wonder it has been changed to UPC-Arena) on 19 September 2002. The team that achieved these exploits had been disbanded and they were rebuilding. Also, their camp had been thrown into turmoil the weekend before our game with the resignation of their long-serving coach Ivica Osim after a run of disappointing results, and they had a caretaker manager.

They showed no sign of these problems on the night, however; maybe the difficulties made them more determined to prove themselves. We coped with them for the first half-hour, thanks to our goalkeeper Broto, who brilliantly blocked a penalty that they were awarded after 20 minutes, but they went one up late in the first half. They came storming out after the break, and we had a dreadful spell in which they smashed in four goals in ten minutes. Determined to salvage something from the game – if only our pride – we kept hammering away while they sat back and defended their lead. It paid off when Rolando Zarate and Stuart Lovell scored in stoppage time – at 5–2, enough to give us a slim chance of pulling off a Houdini-type escape in the second leg at Almondvale.

Zarate was an interesting teammate. When he was on song, he scored some spectacular goals for us, and the bigger the occasion or the more prestigious the opposition, the more he would really turn it on. At only 23, he had gone from Argentina to Real Madrid, where he had been a goal-scorer, but they moved him on to Murcia and since leaving Livi he has played in Saudi Arabia and now Mexico.

He was typical of Livingston's ability to find top-class foreign players willing to come to Scotland, while bigger clubs seemed to miss them. I believe it was down to the management's imaginative approach and not least to the wide-ranging contacts of coaches such as Davie Hay.

We were all disappointed to have gone down so heavily and lost so many goals so quickly in our first proper European match. Between ourselves, we agreed with Jim Leishman, who said we had been a bit naive in allowing opposing players to come off us, giving them a chance to attack the ball. Jim, who always looks for something positive, also reminded us that there was a glimmer of hope and 5–2 was better than 3–0 because of the away goals.

Our home leg against Sturm Graz was a typical Livingston roller-coaster spectacular, full of thrills, drama and passion. Going in with a three-goal deficit, we knew it would take a very special performance to keep us in Europe – and we almost pulled it off.

Our aim was to get enough early goals to scare Sturm Graz into a defensive game and deny them the chance of the all-important away goals. Straight from the kick-off, we had them under pressure, and their goalkeeper was having to come off his line to deal with our forwards in their box.

It started to look good for us when we took the lead after half an hour when Barry Wilson was felled in the box, took the spot-kick himself and sent their goalie the wrong way. But it was too much of a miracle to hope for against a class side like Sturm Graz, and they seemed to have it sewn up when they got two goals, one on either side of the interval.

However, we were not finished yet. One thing that marked out that Livingston side was the never-say-die spirit instilled in us by Jim Leishman and his coaching colleagues. Before Sturm Graz had time to settle into a defensive pattern, we pulled one back when Davide Xausa fired in a volley that gave their keeper no chance.

Then it was my turn. I charged upfield for a set piece, and David Bingham played the ball head-high right into my path. The long, looping header from ten yards out, well clear of their goalie, was one of the most satisfying goals I have ever scored.

That revived the glimmer of hope, and we got the winner in injury-time when Barry Wilson fired in a 25-yard shot for his second goal of the game.

We had some cause for complaint, because Bingham had a goal disallowed for offside and then thought he had forced the ball over the line again with a shot off the underside of the crossbar, but the Norwegian referee waved play on.

The Livi fans certainly got their money's worth, and, as players, we could feel proud. They said it was a famous victory, but the hard truth was that, despite such a magnificent fight-back and proving we were not outclassed at European level, our UEFA Cup dream was over.

It was a double lesson: when you are down, you must

never give up and always keep fighting – but you also have to take your chances.

It was a fantastic experience for the club so early in its history, and it showed how far Livi had come from Meadowbank to Europe. It was a marvellous journey.

Directors, managers, players and fans were all one big happy family at Almondvale, and I also saw how a football family can come together through tragedy. The whole club was shattered when our French striker Eugene Dadi discovered his girlfriend Lydia dead in their home when he got back from training. Jim Leishman was close to tears when he told us, 'We are a family. When one of us hurts, we all hurt.' I prayed for Eugene, hoping that God would give him the right direction and the peace that no man could give him. No one could bring back Lydia, and only God could fill the space where she had been taken from him. These are drastic times, when the Devil tries to take the opportunity to bring negative things to people's lives. To lose his loved one in a foreign land must have been harder than anything you can imagine. We felt we had to be his family, and Eugene must have felt the same, because the very next day he came into the dressing-room before our game against Hibs on the Saturday and made a very moving and emotional speech in which he thanked us all for our support and asked us to go out and do our best. But we could see in his face how badly he was hurting.

To our amazement, Eugene even wanted to play and do well for the team, but, quite rightly, Jim Leishman and the club doctor said he was in no fit state. We all mourned for Eugene, but we had to get on and do our jobs. Not surprisingly, though, we lost 2–1.

If this defeat was understandable, less so was our

general lack of form in the 2002–03 season. At the corresponding time in the previous season, we'd had a 13-game winning run in the SPL and were close behind Rangers and Celtic, but we struggled right from the start of the 2002–03 season. It ended in a frantic scramble between ourselves, Dundee United, Motherwell and Partick Thistle to avoid relegation.

Several times in my football career, I have seen it happen. How can a club that beats all comers and achieves miracles suddenly go into a slump? The players are the same, the management have not changed, the tactics have worked in the past, the opposition is the same standard as it was, but the wins just will not come as they did before – and it is impossible to find an explanation.

It is almost a law of football that after hitting a winning run like that, you inevitably get stuck in a rut. The whole team starts getting jittery, forwards who have been scoring goals cannot find the target and there is uncertainty in defence when what is needed is the old confidence.

We knew we were a better side than our performances suggested, but we just could not seem to get the results – and maybe, in the back of our minds, we were focused on the UEFA campaign.

I was happy with my own performance in defence, especially winning balls in the air, but I wasn't getting on the scoresheet as much as I wanted. For a while, nothing seemed to be going in, as I was hitting the post, the keepers were making good saves and I had a perfectly good goal disallowed against Aberdeen – but I knew if I kept working at it, my scoring average would improve.

I was relieved when it did, just in time to make a difference in our relegation fight. One game against Dundee United was a real cruncher, and I scored probably the best goal of my career. I took the ball from the halfway line, played a one-two with Camacho, took it behind a defender, and when the keeper came out, I slipped it past him. The pitch was so muddy it just trickled along the ground and almost didn't make it into the net.

Towards the end of the season, when every goal was crucial, I headed the second goal in a 3–0 victory over Dundee United and, unusually for me, fired one home with my boot in a 3–0 win over Partick Thistle.

The pattern seemed to be that we would lose goals in the first half, then come into our game and dominate in the second half. One match against Rangers in December was typical, but it also showed that we still had what it took to be a danger against the top-of-the-table teams. Reports said that Rangers paid the penalty for being complacent and slacking off when they got a couple of goals ahead. Maybe – but I can assure you that they were taking no chances on that day because they were only one point behind Celtic and needed to take the full points from us before the following Saturday's Old Firm game.

It may have seemed all over when Rangers were leading 4–0 by half-time, including a hat-trick by Shota Arveladze. What made it worse for me was that the second of Arveladze's goals came when a cross-ball took a slight deflection off me and onto his head.

People ask how a defender feels when he puts in an own goal or accidentally turns the ball onto an opposition player who scores. The answer is simple: bad! But anyone with any knowledge of the game knows that these accidents will happen in a crowded penalty box when the defending team is under pressure. Mind you,

I have seen backs completely lose their heads and make suicidal pass-backs, or forget where their goal is and put the ball in the net when they are sure they are making a safe clearance . . .

Both sides made changes at half-time, and the Livingston substitution turned the game, because Rolando Zarate came on and sent a 30-yard free-kick hurtling past Stefan Klos. Our defender Gary Bollan was sent off in the 75th minute, after receiving a second yellow card, but then Zarate scored a second with three minutes left. It was Rangers' turn to be anxious, and, believe me, they were glad when that final whistle went!

We still had a lot of work to do to make ourselves safe by the end of the season, and things were made worse by a dreadful injury count, which made it impossible to field a settled team.

It came good just in time, and we avoided relegation by beating the other teams that were struggling at the bottom of the Premier League. I have to admit that our 35 points looked pretty puny against the 97 points of Rangers and Celtic. (That was the season the championship was decided by goal difference and Rangers took their 50th league title by a single goal.)

Our 3–1 win over Partick on 3 May 2003 put us into ninth place, just above them on goal difference. We lost 2–1 to Hibs on 17 May, and then a suffered a 6–2 defeat to Motherwell for our last game of the season, but by then we had done enough to claw ourselves out of the relegation zone. Bottom-placed Motherwell were saved from the drop by a controversial decision that prevented Falkirk from coming up because of their proposed ground-share with Airdrie.

Strangely, I felt that fighting against relegation and

learning as a club how to stay in the top division made me a better player. It made me stronger mentally and improved my all-round game. What really pleased me was to be voted Player of the Year by the Livingston fans.

One reporter wrote:

> If the Old Firm continue their policy of buying players who've done the business against them, like Claudio Caniggia, Russell Latapy, Didier Agathe or Momo Sylla, then Andrews may well not be in West Lothian for too much longer.

I didn't pay much attention to that at the time, but his words were to prove prophetic . . .

The 2003–04 season turned out to be my last with Livingston – and it was also one of the strangest I have experienced. Once again, the Livi Lions reached astonishing heights that were matched by desperate lows and behind-the-scenes dramas. And I was in the headlines for letting my faith decide my footballing future.

Ian McCall of Dundee United – a manager I greatly admire – made a £300,000 bid for myself and Barry Wilson. He was in the middle of the 'Tannadice revolution' and had signed nine players, including my countrymen Collin Samuel from Falkirk and Jason Scotland from the Defence Force club back home in Trinidad.

Livingston's general manager Davie Hay said the club would prefer to keep me for football reasons, but they could do with the money and might have to lose me for financial reasons. They valued me at £400,000, and there was a lot of toing and froing, fuelled by press speculation.

I knew the day would come when I would have to

move to a bigger club, but God is the controller of my life. I prayed and asked God for wisdom before I went to Tannadice for the transfer talks on my personal terms. I was praying every day for guidance, and I was content to wait until He told me what the right move was. There was a lot of disbelief and, yes, ridicule when I said, 'If God directs me to stay, then that is what I will do. It won't matter how much money I am offered or what Ian McCall says to persuade me. God will never lead me down the wrong path, and I will do what is right.'

Because of their financial need, Livi agreed a fee for me, which I believe was £250,000. As before, when I said that faith had helped me to overcome injury, there was a lot of mockery when I turned down the offer, even though it would have meant more money for me. With Livingston in administration, my rejection of it on the grounds of my belief really surprised everyone. The Tannadice management issued a statement saying my decision was due to 'other forces', which showed they did not really understand.

Ian McCall respected my belief, but I know that deep in his heart he thought it was a very strange reason. In all his career as a manager, no one had told him such a thing. He was kind enough to say, 'People might want to have fun with this, but in my view it is a serious issue and one we have to respect. He's turned our offer down for serious reasons.

'It had nothing to do with Dundee United and everything to do with his own beliefs. We absolutely respect that. It really is that simple.

'His faith has guided him this far. He has prayed and come to a decision, and while it is obviously not the one that we want, we wish him well. Marvin may well wear the tangerine of this club in the future, but just not at this precise moment.'

After I had refused the move to Dundee United, we knocked them out of the CIS Cup, beating them 1–0 on their home ground on 29 October 2003. They had dominated the game, but the only goal of the match came from a hotly disputed free-kick awarded when I was pulled down on the halfway line. From it, Stuart Lovell crashed a shot off the crossbar, which hit goalie Paul Gallacher on the back and bounced into his own net. In the match programme, Ian McCall had joked that he hoped God would be on his side to even things up after throwing a spanner in the works of the transfer bid!

The Dundee United fans were less forgiving, and the next time we played them at Almondvale, they booed me every time I touched the ball and gave me a lot of banter. I was not really bothered because I didn't expect them to be happy about me rejecting them.

My belief in God's power came into play again in September 2003, when another serious injury threatened to put me out of the game. In a home match against Kilmarnock, I went up for a header and came down in a tangle with an opponent, landing with my arm under me. I had no chance to pull it out to break my fall, and it took my full weight. I knew the shoulder was seriously damaged, and a sports-injury specialist said it was more like a typical rugby injury. The bones had separated from the muscle, and the ligaments had been overstretched. His prediction was that it would be a minimum of six weeks before it healed sufficiently for me to play.

I went to the church to pray with Pastor Joe, and again God healed me miraculously. There was real astonishment when I was back training the next week, and I was back on the team-sheet after a couple of weeks. I played with some strapping on the shoulder, just in case I damaged it again, but it was fine and has not troubled me since.

Livingston's owner Dominic Keane and manager Jim Leishman both thought big, and there was no limit to what they would try in their ambition to bring success to the club. Unfortunately, one bold experiment went badly wrong and caused a great deal of unhappiness – but you cannot blame them for trying.

We were all excited when, in June 2003, they brought in Marcio Maximo Barcellos, the first Brazilian coach to be put in charge of a British team. He came with an impressive history behind him: as a youth coach, he had discovered and developed superstars like Ronaldo and Ronaldinho in Brazil, and he came to us from the Grand Cayman Islands, where he was technical coach. He replaced Jim Leishman, who became general manager at the club, while Davie Hay continued as a consultant with the first team.

There was no reason why the set-up should not have worked, because most major teams have a sizeable coaching staff. But, at Livingston, it seemed there were a lot of strong personalities with different responsibilities and different ideas, and Maximo was a newcomer among people who had built up the club from nothing. Perhaps that is why it all went sour so quickly.

When a new gaffer arrives, it is always an unsettling time for players, but, as far as we were concerned, he had our full support. It helped that, on the day before the players met our new coach, Dominic Keane called a meeting to explain his thinking. Something like that has not happened in my experience before or since. The players had been worried by rumours that Jim Leishman and Davie Hay might be leaving, and it showed how important Maximo's coming was to the chairman. The first thing that struck me was the obvious concern shown in making sure we were fully informed of why the changes had been made, and, in particular, how Dominic had gone about identifying the right candidate. In 13 years in professional football, this was my first experience of being 'kept in the loop', and I thought it was an important gesture that would go a long way to quelling the rumours about our managerial future.

The new coach changed a lot of things and brought in a new regime, which was good for us all and made us think a lot more about ourselves as professionals and how we played the game. Initially, most of us found it difficult to adapt to Maximo's coaching methods. For one thing, he had us on the training ground for longer shifts and increased the work pattern from two sessions a day to three. It made sense, because the old method of training for the 90-minute length of a game was obviously not enough; the coach explained to us that the team with extra stamina, fitness and understanding of each other would win more games.

Another of his big ideas was to have a less rigid game plan and more flair and fluidity depending on how play was going. He believed that a competent team should be able to change formation and adapt tactics in mid-match to cope with the circumstances that crop up.

He was also a very fair man to work for and spoke to us as fellow professionals, preferring us to call him 'coach'. Some coaches can be pretty rough with their tongues, but that was not Maximo's way, and by the start of the season we felt we were well prepared and could get back the form we had shown in that exciting first season in the SPL.

We made a stuttering start to the season with a disappointing opening-day 1–1 draw against Partick Thistle, but, after a couple of wins, the chairman and board seemed relaxed that Maximo's methods would work. However, there was no disguising the fact that there were rows going on in the background amongst the coaching staff.

Even so, it was a complete shock when Maximo resigned in October. He said it was for deeply serious private reasons and he was returning home with no other job lined up.

The chairman seemed truly upset and said our results under the coach – two league wins, three draws and three defeats, plus getting into the third round of the CIS Cup – were not an issue. The coach had said it would take eight or nine competitive games in the league and the team would come good. That seemed true, because our last three games under him were solid performances, with two wins, including a 3–0 victory over Aberdeen at Pittodrie, and a draw.

Tension had been building up at Almondvale for a couple of weeks, and, unknown to us at the time, Maximo had gone to the chairman on the eve of that Aberdeen game asking to be released from his one-year contract. Dominic Keane had persuaded him to take another couple of weeks to think about it, but he could not change the coach's mind because it was 'something that is outside football'.

The players were all disappointed to be losing the

coach because we felt we had benefited from his presence, individually and as a team, and some got quite emotional. To me, it showed what I already knew from my experience: the Scottish game is different and it takes time to accustom yourself. To be fair to Maximo, as well as making demands on us to change, he was also adapting his ideas to suit the Scottish style.

Three years later, I had that 'we've been here before' feeling when a similar thing happened to Paul Le Guen at Rangers: a new manager from another country trying to introduce new methods, a new style and a new attitude, and failing to carry the dressing-room and back-room staff with him . . .

Davie Hay and the first-team coach, Allan Preston, were back in charge for the next game. Davie had been on holiday, and Maximo insisted that the relationship between himself and Davie had been a normal and professional one. Allan Preston admitted to having had some differences of opinion with Maximo but said that had nothing to do with his departure.

Both of them, and Billy Kirkwood, the Under-21 coach, were definite that the chairman had been right to take a gamble on Maximo. We all wished him well; we knew there would always be a future in football for such a man, and he has since been appointed head coach of the Tanzania national team.

It had been an interesting and exciting few months, but it had also been very unsettling – especially for me, with the speculation over my move to Dundee United.

The so-called 'January sales', when the transfer window opens and the market in players in Scotland gets hectic, added to my uncertainty. I was due to become a free agent in June, but Jim Leishman had been saying to me that people were noticing I was even more consistent that season and it was only a matter of time before the transfer speculation started up again. He expected one of the big clubs to come in for me and said that Livingston would like to keep me but, in the post-Bosman climate, it would be a question of taking the money while I was still under contract.

I was being compared with stars such as Bobo Balde at Celtic and Lorenzo Amoruso at Rangers, and all I knew was that I wanted to be up there at the highest level competing against the very best.

The Maximo affair showed how Dominic Keane had always been prepared to pay the price to get the right man, whether he be a coach or a player. With attendances of around 7,000 per game at a superb new 10,000-seater stadium built to meet the SPL regulations, the club's, finances were being stretched, and, without us knowing, the overdraft reached a crippling £3.5 million.

The blow fell in February 2004, on the eve of another big match for the club – the CIS Cup semi-final against Dundee at Easter Road. The entire club staff were called together and given the news that Livingston were going into administration. The bankers were calling in their loans, and Dominic Keane said he would have to give up the club. He was in tears in front of the whole squad and kept repeating, 'They've failed me, they've failed me.' He just had to put up his hands and say, 'I've got to give up the club.'

Many of the players just did not believe it because we were still getting paid and having a good run in the CIS Cup, which was bound to bring in extra money. It was hardly the best preparation for an important semi-final to be told that, after the game, some players would not be at the club . . .

But they had to make ends meet. The administrators were coming into Almondvale, and players on good wages who were not regulars would have to go. That certainly made it a tense game!

In the early stages, Nacho Novo – who was then making his reputation as a fast and tricky striker – caused us a lot of problems. In the back three, we had to be constantly on the alert as he seemed to be everywhere in our half, looking to pounce on a loose ball. The Dundee fans were trying everything and put up a big shout for hand ball when I brought the ball down with my body; it was rightly not given, but Nacho was on it in a flash and managed to snap a shot just wide of our goal.

For the rest of the game, we were playing frenetic end-to-end stuff and the Livingston fans were singing their hearts out. I was praying for a miracle, and my prayers were answered. In the very last minute, we got a penalty when Fernando Pasquinelli was sandwiched and bundled over by the Dundee central defenders as he raced into the box. I was standing on the pitch, just asking, 'Please, God, help us through this hard time. Bless us with this penalty.'

Our striker Derek Lilley kept his cool and hit a superb penalty kick. The Dundee keeper Julian Speroni was a Christian as well, but I guess my prayer was stronger than his . . .

The Livi fans went crazy because it meant that, although in deep turmoil, their team had reached their first cup final. After all that, there had to be a future for Livingston. Didn't there?

But the very next day, seven of the players, who had not

been expecting it, were told they were going. Six of us – skipper Stuart Lovell, Alan Main, Emmanuel Dorado, Oscar Rubio, Fernando Pasquinelli and myself – agreed to take a cut in wages to help the club.

The administrators moved into the club office at noon that very day. I confess I will never understand how football finances always seem to be in a state of crisis at club after club, even when they are providing entertainment, doing well on the field and have a loyal following. As Dominic Keane said, 'Football has got a very serious illness called debt . . .'

With all that going on, the odds seemed against us for the final on 14 March, versus a young Hibs side who had beaten Rangers on penalties in their semi-final. We were even outnumbered on the Hampden terraces, because seven thousand of our faithful supporters had made the journey against four times as many from Edinburgh.

It was the first time I had played at Hampden, and it was something to see at one end of the ground a little bit of yellow, our fans wearing the Livingston colours, and all round the green of Hibernian.

It was a really devastating time, because some tremendous players had been released immediately after winning the semi-final. At least the management kept faith with them, gave them tickets to the final and allowed them to come into the dressing-room at Hampden – although, if it had been me, I am not sure how I would have felt about being so close but denied the chance to go on the field.

I was in constant prayer, asking God for help, saying, 'God, God, you've taken us to this final – help us through it.' We had been underdogs all the way, and everyone knew the club was down and in trouble.

Hibs were pressing us, because they were confident, while we were tense and worried. For a number of our guys, it was the first big occasion, the first final, in their careers, and it took time for our confidence to build. I had to clear one off the line from Garry O'Connor after a couple of minutes, and I can tell you we were mightily relieved to go in 0–0 at half-time.

Davie Hay gave us the encouragement we needed. He just told us, 'Guys, we're still in this game, and it's there for us to win. We were scared and timid in the first half, but we still came through. Just go out there and express yourselves. If we play to our capabilities, we are going to win this game.'

When we went out for the second half, we were a much better side and hit them with two goals in two minutes. First, Burton O'Brien collected the ball, took it to the byline, dummied a Hibs defender and made a great cutback to Derek Lilley, who side-footed it into the net. I was just looking to the skies and thanking the Lord, saying, 'God is so good.' Before you knew it, David Fernandez played a glorious pass to my fellow defender Jamie McAllister, who broke out from our half and cracked a low shot past the Hibs goalie Daniel Andersson. By this time, I was simply asking myself, 'Oh, my goodness – is this really happening?'

With all this excitement, I went into one tackle and twisted my ankle. I was limping, and I just kept repeating to myself, 'I'm not coming off – I am not coming off in this game.' I was defending for my life and praying.

I looked up at the scoreboard, and it said 90 minutes, Livingston 2 Hibs 0, but the referee played some stoppage-time, and every minute was agony. At the final whistle, I went down on my knees, and tears were coming from my eyes, because we had won that CIS Cup in a time of torment and trouble.

It was football history, Livingston's first-ever national trophy, and one of the greatest days of my life. But it was a mixture of joy and tragedy, because the club was in such disarray and some good friends and teammates were having to leave.

At the same time, it was the finest way for the team to pay back Dominic Keane, Davie Hay and Jim Leishman for all they had done in taking the club from obscurity to the very top. The newspapers said, quite rightly, it was a triumph over adversity and a football fairytale.

Davie, a former Celtic player and manager who played for Scotland in the 1974 World Cup, said this day of glory with a new team from a new town topped any of his previous football achievements. He deserved full credit for showing such strength and leadership in not just holding us together but also taking us to such a success.

I knew that, no matter what happened in my football career, I would never forget that day. It showed me how great God is and that, at such a time of trouble, He was with me and with the club.

I treasure the picture taken in the stadium of us celebrating with the team and the Livingston fans together. I took off my Livingston strip and underneath, for all to see, was the T-shirt I always wear saying 'With God Nothing Is Impossible'.

Only four days later, we were back in action against Aberdeen in a Scottish Cup quarter-final replay at Almondvale. I passed a late fitness test for the ankle injury I had picked up in the CIS final, and the question was whether we could stay on a high from Hampden or whether it had drained us.

We got great encouragement from the Livi fans, who gave us a standing ovation as we ran onto the pitch, and that gave us a such a lift that it carried us through. The priority was to progress to the semi-final, which would ensure another big pay day, which would help the club's finances.

It was not a pretty performance, but it was gutsy, and we held on after Burton O'Brien scored a typically well-taken opportunist goal in the 26th minute. The media summed it up: 'Hay's team were running on empty for much of the game, but O'Brien's strike and the sheer tenacity of a five-man defence, organised by the indefatigable Marvin Andrews, combined to secure Livi's victory.'

Thus, in April 2004, Livingston went back to Hampden for the Scottish Cup semi-final against Celtic. It would have been stretching the fairytale too far to expect us to win against a Martin O'Neill side who had the treble in their sights and were preparing for a UEFA Cup quarter-final tie against Villareal.

The Celtic manager paid Livingston the compliment of fielding his strongest side and declaring that we and the tournament were worthy of respect. In the end, although we were by no means disgraced, they had a comfortable 3–1 win, with two goals by Chris Sutton and one from Henrik Larsson against a consolation goal for us by Colin McMenamin.

I was disappointed about Sutton's opening goal because the ball took an unlucky bounce off one of our players for Larsson to put Sutton through. The change of direction had me going the wrong way, and Sutton had time to sidestep and slip the ball into the net. Against such quality opposition, you can't afford to have even one break going against you, and we were unsuccessfully chasing the game after that.

The defeat did not spoil what was a fabulous achievement. For a club in administration to win one national trophy and reach the semi-final of another was really astonishing. We were told that the CIS Insurance Cup prize money, turnstile takings and television revenues would probably put £500,000 into the club coffers, and the Scottish Cup run provided another welcome windfall. But the truth was that it made only a dent in Livingston's huge debt.

From the start of the year, I knew I was playing on borrowed time at Livingston. For months, the word – even back in Trinidad – was that I would be following in the footsteps of my fellow-Trinidadian Russell Latapy and going to Rangers.

Allan Preston, then coach at Livingston, was talking up my prospects and saying I was the right player to help Rangers' defensive problems. Allan gave a very frank assessment of my capabilities – good and bad! He said, 'Marvin is the best at what he does in Scotland, and I include Bobo Balde in that. Don't ask him to hit 60-yard passes onto the toes of David Fernandez, but if you want the ball won in the air or on the ground, then he'll do it for you. He's a fantastic player, and he's captain of his country. He's got faults, but his attitude is spot-on. He's very fair, and there's not a malicious bone in his body, and other managers always mention him after we play them. I'm not trying to tell other clubs how to pick their team, but if you see Rangers are without Moore and Khizanishvili, then maybe they need a stopper like Marvin.'

Then he dropped a very heavy hint, given Livingston's

money crisis: 'It wouldn't surprise me if other clubs come in for him when the transfer window opens. Obviously, we don't want to lose him, but from a business point of view, if a bid came in for him, then we might need to because he's our most valuable asset. The chairman would know better than me if the club does need the money and Marvin does need to be sold, but money's tight for everybody at the moment.

'If ever a man deserves a move to a bigger club, then it's Marvin. He's just turned 28 and he's got the best years of his playing career just ahead of him. And he's honest enough to admit that he doesn't see himself at Livingston forever and he wants to play at the top.'

He was right when he said that. I had turned down Dundee United, but, even when I was doing well at Livingston and getting a lot of attention, I always felt it was a stepping stone for me. I believed God would promote me to bigger things and I'd reach greater heights, similar to my two friends Dwight Yorke and Russell Latapy. I supported Liverpool as a boy and at an early stage in my career hoped it would be my destiny to play for them, if God willed it. But the great Glasgow Rangers would do very nicely . . .

So it was no surprise when Alex McLeish came in for me in April 2004, and I signed a pre-agreement with Rangers to join in the summer. I was on a free transfer, which must have made the deal more attractive for him. Livingston confirmed I would be free to go at the end of the season, which had been fixed when I'd agreed to take a wage cut earlier in the season.

Ironically, the deal was done in the week that Livingston played Rangers at Almondvale and forced a 1–1 draw. As always, I gave everything for the jersey I was wearing;

I had a real tussle with striker Stevie Thompson and, unfortunately, he ended up with a sore head after we clashed in an aerial duel. No wonder Stevie said when I joined Ibrox that I was a very physical player who was difficult to play against!

Alex McLeish had also signed the French star Jean-Alain Boumsong, another dominant defender, from Auxerre on a similar pre-contract and free transfer, and he spelt out the job we were expected to do: 'There has been criticism over the last couple of years and beyond my time at Rangers that we have been lacking a physical presence. We know we are not physical enough, and we have tried to put that right. I've seen countless balls into the box that we haven't dealt with as well as we should have, and we have lost goals at set pieces to other teams as well, not just Celtic. It's up to Marvin whether he can fix that, but I do think he will be a useful player.'

We won my last game for Livingston 2–1, and it was a very emotional match for me. I never expected to see 10,000 people standing up in my honour. Nobody left the stadium; they all stayed behind to pay tribute to what I had done for the club, and I took a lap round the pitch, just feeling the warmth of the Livingston family.

You get all sorts of honours in football – but that truly was an honour.

Chapter Four

THE RANGERS MIRACLE

When I joined Rangers at the age of 28, I knew I would have to work hard to prove myself and win the approval of the Ibrox fans. Their reaction to my signing had been lukewarm, perhaps because of the games I had played for Livingston against Rangers.

I knew there would be snipers waiting in the wings just for Marvin Andrews to make a mistake or stumble or give away a goal. I prayed for guidance to deal with the people waiting to say negative things about me.

My attitude has always been that sometimes I might have a bad game. The Lord made me human and not perfect. The media may highlight a mistake, and people may say what they want, but I know every time I am going on the pitch that I am going to give my all and do my best.

Opposition is natural in life – not everybody is going to say, 'Ah, he is going to be great.' When people say you can't do something, and you know deep down in your heart that you can, you must overcome obstacles to achieve your goals. That is how winners and champions are made.

They were saying that, with a pool of players which included defenders such as Zurab Khizanishvili, Craig Moore, Jean-Alain Boumsong and Bob Malcolm, I would be little more than a squad player. I believed I was going to play every week.

It was becoming clear to me, from all the amazing things that had happened in my life, that God was taking me stage by stage. He doesn't just rush you straight through, He trains you and prepares you, and I believe that the sky is the limit for Marvin Andrews. Even while I was playing out the season at Livingston, I was given a taste of the feelings that Rangers players can stir up among supporters of other clubs. After it was known I would be going to Ibrox, we went to Aberdeen, where I had always got a good reception, and their fans singled me out for abuse.

I had been told there was a real feud between Aberdeen and Rangers, but I had no idea it was so fierce, and I still have no idea what it is about. It did not bother me because it was just football and just fans who needed someone to shout at. It must be because of something that happened years ago. I quite enjoy this kind of rivalry, as long as it is healthy and does not get out of proportion, with verbal abuse and violence. I was not quite sure where the Old Firm games against Celtic fitted into that. It just seemed strange to me that two sets of supporters could go into that game each claiming God is on their side – while screaming un-Christian-like hatred at each other.

When we played pre-season matches in Austria and Moscow and against Tottenham Hotspur, I got some idea of the devotion of the Rangers supporters. Even though they were only friendlies, the travelling support was astonishing, and I discovered there is actually a huge Rangers support in Austria. That was when I first realised how big a club I had joined, and that is a great incentive for a young player. Everything was there: training and medical facilities, great back-room support, a huge fan base, and, of course, Rangers FC is an iconic club.

It was all so completely different from Livingston, who had come up through the divisions, made a name for themselves, fought through financial crisis and struggled to get established in the SPL. The expectation was much higher, so there was more pressure to perform well, and you were expected to win every game. There were other pressures from being part of such a famous club. Everybody knows you are a Rangers player, so you are always under the microscope – but I think that is good for you, because it makes you think about what you do in your personal life.

Rangers help their new players with housing, and there were some comments when I turned down the chance of a quite luxurious home in very nice surroundings. But I have always been happy in Kirkcaldy because my church, the Zion Praise Centre, is there, and that is the most important thing to me. It did not make sense to me to leave all that fellowship when I could easily travel to training every day.

People seemed to think it unbelievable that I refused the offer of a luxury home near my other Ibrox teammates. It took an hour to drive to training sessions in Glasgow, but I didn't mind that, and Rangers didn't have a problem with it either.

That first season was full of fantastic achievement for the club and for myself. Even some of my teammates admitted later that they did not think I would be a good signing for them, but my attitude was that God was responsible for me going to Rangers and He would help me prove those people wrong.

You can imagine how I felt at the end of the season to be a first-team regular who had helped Rangers win the championship and CIS Cup and even to have scored four times. I was Player of the Year, and that was even more special for me, because it was the players' choice and my fellow professionals were confirming that I had performed at that high level.

It was a great irony that my first competitive game for Rangers was in the SPL against Livingston. After playing my heart out for them for two years, I was suddenly on the opposing side. Livingston actually came to Ibrox as SPL leaders! True, only one game had been played and they were on top by goal difference, but they were obviously up for the game. No quarter was given by either side, and, although the Rangers tackling was forceful, my old teammates showed they could also hand it out.

I was happy in one sense that I didn't score against my old team, but I did my job and didn't allow their strikers to score in what turned out to be a 4–0 hammering. The game also showed that, although I was wearing another team's jersey, there was still a relationship with the Livi fans. It was a bit emotional because there was a warm greeting, and I stood there at the end of the game and we applauded each other.

Before my first game in the blue strip against Celtic, I was excited. And when religion is dragged into it, the event becomes even more passionate. The religion involved in the Old Firm game has nothing to do with God and the Bible. It is a man-made thing. In Scotland, religion and believing are two separate things. Until I came to Scotland, I had no idea how religion and football were all mixed up together and how club rivalry also meant sectarian rivalry. I was surprised and shocked by it, and I do not think it is healthy; it is bad for religion, bad for the community and bad for football. To me, the 'religion' that is associated with the Old Firm has nothing to do with the Almighty God. The traditional Rangers–Celtic thing is not spiritual and has no connection with principles or the Lord Jesus Christ. Being Catholic or Protestant should mean something deeper, but to many it is all to do with football, and these people don't go by what the Bible says. If there was no Old Firm, they would find other ways to show their bigotry – and that is a perversion of faith. It is incredible that so-called religious belief can lead to violence on the terraces and the street and has even led to the loss of young lives. My God is not a god of violence; He tells us to love our neighbours. From what I have heard, the violence has since calmed down a little, but there is still too much of it.

I kept trying to tell Rangers and Celtic people that there is nothing wrong with loving your team and supporting it with enthusiasm; as a player, I admit I have been uplifted on the field when I've heard the fans getting behind me. But there is a whole world of difference between that and hate-filled bigotry.

I've been heartened by seeing a husband and wife, one in a Celtic top and the other in a Rangers top, and one of the greatest things you can see is kids playing together in the park in different Old Firm strips – that is the way we should go in the future. Wearing blue or green colours does not make you a different kind of human being, to hate or be hated.

My concern, from being in it and around it, is when I see a little boy or girl coming to a game with their mum or dad or aunt or uncle and hearing that older relative saying obscene and abusive words when they see a Rangers or Celtic player. They think, 'Mum and Dad say these things, so it's OK for me to say them.'

A seven or ten year old shouting obscene language at a grown man in a Rangers or Celtic jersey has no idea what he is saying. He has absorbed this language in his home and his neighbourhood, and it is planted in his heart and mind. He has heard people saying, literally, 'I hate Rangers' or 'I hate Celtic'. That is how hatred grows and spreads. It is poisoning the minds and breeding hatred in the young who will be adults in ten or twenty years, so that it continues for generation after generation. They are going to grow up with that same hatred. That is the cycle that has to be broken.

Every Old Firm derby is critical. It doesn't matter what else has happened in the season, in the past weeks or months, and it isn't really about sending a message to the other team. Each time Rangers and Celtic meet, that match is something all by itself.

You know it's the oldest derby in the world, and there is nothing else in football like it. Not even the famous derbies in the English Premiership, such as Arsenal and Tottenham, Manchester United and City, or Liverpool and Everton, come close to electrifying a nation like the Old Firm.

My first Old Firm game was set up in the media as me versus John Hartson, the burly, bustling Welsh international forward who had tied a Celtic club record by scoring in four successive derbies. We were two big guys coming up against each other, and I knew we would have a good tussle when we met. I respected the challenge posed by John, who is a very good player – strong, physical and aggressive – although you would never expect him to beat you for pace. I have to say I prefer to face strong, direct target men rather than the speedy, more subtle attackers. I have never had any special tactics for dealing with either type of forward. I just have to be aggressive and win the ball from them.

Some people thought it strange when I spoke up for one of the Celtic team, but I always reckoned there was not much difference between me and the Celtic defender Bobo Balde. It was even suggested in print that people would like to see us playing side by side in the same defence. How scary would that be for strikers? You'd have to ask them . . .

Bobo always seemed to come in for a lot more criticism, and it was wrong for fans and writers to label him a dirty player. Hard and physical, yes, but that is our game. I should know, because my whole game has been based around doing the same things as Bobo, and that includes winning headers in the air and sometimes flying into tackles. I have made a successful club and international career using a similar style to the one Bobo has employed for Celtic, and I do not see much difference in our approach. Nobody has ever called me a dirty player; in fact, quite the opposite, and I have been praised for my aggressive and defensive play.

There were one or two unsavoury incidents with Bobo, including a charge of elbowing a Hibs player in the face, but I thought everything Bobo did got blown out of all proportion, especially when he was newly arrived from France and still adapting to the Scottish game.

It was the same when I publicly praised Henrik Larsson, who will always rank in my book as one of Europe's – if not the world's – top strikers. All of us in the SPL were privileged to have a player like him, and it was always a pleasure to play against someone who has achieved so much in the game. Playing against top stars like Henrik certainly improved my game, because I knew that if I wanted to get better, I would have to match them. You knew that all they needed was one chance and it would be a goal. I used to watch him on the TV highlights and hope that one day I would get a chance to play on the same pitch as him. Henrik now has extra experience, but he has always been special – and not just because of his scoring ability. He shields the ball as well as anyone I have ever played against. He always gets his body between the opponent and the ball, and any defender who tries to get to it has to foul him. The other impressive thing about Henrik is his attitude: although he is the greatest of goal-getters and people always expect more from him, he never lets the pressure get to him. He does not care so much if he does not score, because the most important thing to him is the team.

I wasn't chosen for the first Old Firm game of the 2004–05 season against Celtic at Ibrox, and I took it that Alex McLeish was trying to find the right blend of the new players he had signed in the close season. Celtic won with a stunning strike from Alan Thompson in the 85th minute. Ominously, it was their seventh consecutive Old Firm win, and Rangers had not won at Parkhead for five years. Because of that, there was a lot of criticism of Alex McLeish and the signings he had made.

It was a big relief that in the next two games in quick succession against Celtic, Alex got his reward for the signings he had made – including myself.

My first Old Firm game was a CIS Cup quarter-final, which we won 2–1 in extra-time. It really was the end of the jinx, because we beat them a second time just ten days later in the league. The CIS Cup tie ended that seven-match losing streak against Celtic. What made it ironic was that a few months beforehand there had been a newspaper 'exclusive' that Martin O'Neill was 'ready to step in with a bid of £1.2 million' for me!

It was a marvellous match, and the build-up was such that I regarded it as the most important of my career to that date. It wasn't just John Hartson I had to cope with, for at various stages I was up against the Brazilian maestro Juninho and Henri Camara of Senegal. While I was meant to be watching Hartson, it was Juninho who kept singling me out and then retreating to draw me out of defence and create a gap. I knew not to take the bait and keep our shape at the back. When Celtic seemed unwilling to commit numbers in attack, it also meant Juninho did not have too many options for his pinpoint passing. But it almost misfired when I put in a heavy shoulder charge on him and gave away a free-kick in a dangerous position, from which Hartson narrowly missed with a downward header. And, early in the second half, from a corner, Hartson stole a yard and headed the ball well clear of Stefan Klos, our goalkeeper and captain.

The Celtic fans, who had been a bit quiet, erupted and started singing 'Same old Celtic, always winning'. They became even more cock-a-hoop when their team started playing possession football, with their supporters shouting 'Olé' at every pass.

But we had the last laugh when their over-confidence made them sloppy. A loose pass from Alan Thompson just 20 yards from goal led to a Hamed Namouchi shot being blocked by Celtic's goalie David Marshall, but the ball rolled to Dado Prso to knock it in.

That was a reprieve for us, and we were not going to waste it. In extra-time, Shota Arveladze, who had come on as a substitute, scored with a left-foot shot in the 100th minute, and this time it was the turn of the Rangers fans to sing: 'Can you hear the Celtic sing? No, no . . .'

I remember it so clearly because it was a truly memorable occasion for me and I loved every second of it. The fans, the atmosphere and everything surrounding the game were simply fantastic, and I knew I had achieved something very special in playing for Rangers.

The next game ten days later – maybe too soon for tempers to settle – showed me how high feelings could run. If Rangers could beat Celtic a second time, it would close the gap at the top of the SPL to one point. Everyone was wound up for the game, which was tense, emotional and stormy – and a lot of bad things happened.

After just 15 minutes, our Spanish striker Nacho Novo was tripped in the box by Joos Valgaeren and scored from the penalty spot. Nacho might not have been playing because he had received a red card the previous week, but luckily for us it was downgraded to a yellow and he was able to play against Celtic. Half an hour later, Dado Prso made it 2–0 when he headed in from 12 yards after a Fernando Ricksen free-kick, and we settled in to defend our lead.

Things deteriorated in the second half, and the game got out of hand. Celtic were reduced to ten men when Thompson head-butted Peter Lovenkrands, and Sutton followed for two bookable offences, both hand balls, in quick succession. Bob Malcolm, who had been on Rangers' substitutes' bench, was led up the tunnel by police. He had been celebrating the way the game was going in our favour, but the police interpreted it as an obscene gesture. By the end of the game, three Rangers and four Celts had been booked, as well as the two sendings-off. Even with nine men, Celtic managed to threaten, and we were glad to walk off the field still two goals up. The 50,000 crowd certainly got their money's worth – and I got a lesson on the passion generated by the Old Firm.

The SPL title race in the 2004–05 season was simply astonishing. To begin with, it looked as if we would be trailing behind all the way. Then there was a remarkable Rangers revival, culminating in the most dramatic last day of the season in Scottish football history.

Alex McLeish began the season by trying out several combinations of the players he had signed during the summer. It meant that it took more than a month before I started to get a regular start in the first team. That period of adjustment was not good for results. Meanwhile, the fans were impatient and the media were – as usual – highly critical. With players like Dado Prso, Nacho Novo, Fernando Ricksen, Barry Ferguson and Thomas Buffel in the squad, we were capable of creating loads of chances, but we were not finishing them off.

We won just two of our first seven games in all competitions and had a poor scoring record in away matches early in the season. By mid-September, we were seven points behind Celtic, and Aberdeen and Kilmarnock were above us. Already, it was being openly said and written that Rangers' season was over because we would never make up that gap!

Although everyone knew that the manager was rebuilding the side, there was not much sympathy from the outside. However, the players all believed that, with the squad he had put together, it would come good.

Just a couple of weeks later, we turned the corner with a 2–0 win against Kilmarnock at Ibrox, in which I got my first goal for Rangers and got the Man of the Match award. From a Fernando Ricksen corner, the ball came out of a ruck of players handily for me to jab it over the line from six yards. I was sure I had got another when I had a header blocked and followed up with a shot, but Alan Combe in the Killie goal brought off a terrific double save.

And we really got back into the league race in late October when Celtic surprisingly went down 2–3 to Aberdeen; we beat Dunfermline on the same day, and a couple of days later we thrashed the same Aberdeen side 5–0 at Ibrox. As far as the players were concerned, that was the complete answer to all the doubting fans and critics who had been so negative since the start of the season.

Confidence swept through the club. It put us on an unbeaten run of 16 games and we were at the top of the Premier League. Everybody at Rangers believed that that was our rightful place, but we had not been in the number-one spot for over a year. Things were kept interesting because occasionally we faltered, due to a pile-up of injuries and the draining effect of UEFA and CIS Cup campaigns on top of the League battle.

With ourselves and Celtic playing nip and tuck at the top, every Old Firm game became even more crucial. The meeting at Parkhead in February 2005 was an especially edgy affair, but we came out 2–0 on top. What made it extra-special was that it was Alex McLeish's first victory at Celtic Park, and it was due to the tactical changes he made at half-time.

After the previous meeting, when tempers had boiled over on and off the pitch, we were all on our best behaviour for the first half, which ended without a goal

– and without a caution or even a questionable tackle. In the interval, the boss told us to press them harder. Perhaps I took him too much at his word, because I was shown the yellow card after five minutes! Mind you, Bobo Balde at the other end just beat me to it . . .

We were able to thwart Celtic's best efforts, and the match turned on a terrific save by Ronald Waterreus, who had taken over in Rangers' goal from Stefan Klos. In a typical Celtic move, Chris Sutton dummied and slipped the ball to John Hartson for what looked like a certain score. When Waterreus blocked it from point-blank range, I was close enough to see John Hartson's absolute amazement.

I had a hand in making it a frustrating afternoon for Hartson when he was getting ready to head in a free-kick from inside our six-yard box. I was marking him closely at the set pieces, and threw myself forward to get my header in first. After that, the attacking fire went out of Celtic, and goals by Gregory Vignal and Nacho Novo gave us the victory that put us three points ahead of them.

I am not superstitious, but 13 March was certainly unlucky for me. The newspapers were now looking for every opportunity to mention my faith – which I thought was a good thing, because at least it meant they were mentioning religion – and the headlines after a 2–0 win over Dundee at Dens Park said things such as 'Andrews' belief puts Rangers on road to salvation' and 'Marvin Andrews the answer to Rangers' prayers'.

The reason was that, after only scraping a draw against Inverness Caley Thistle, we were not doing well against Dundee, and Celtic had a couple of games in hand. We could not afford to drop any points, but we were making heavy weather of it until I got a goal nine minutes from time through a header from Fernando Ricksen's corner. And, as Dundee pushed forward to salvage the draw, Fernando got another to sew up the three points.

Despite scoring an important goal, the match was unlucky for me because of an injury which put my entire future at risk. Just after I scored, I went into a challenge on Stevie Lovell, and when I tackled him, he fell badly on top of me. His weight pushed my left knee backwards, far beyond its ability to bend.

I felt excruciating pain, but all my playing career I have believed that I can ignore it and play on. Some knocks might be really sore but I can run them off. I have had worse-looking injuries, including during a game for Livingston against Motherwell where I had a very bad gash over my eye and continued playing, although I needed three different tops because the bleeding was so bad. I didn't know this injury was that serious, just another bad blow that would wear off. I told the physio, 'I'll be OK. I'll try to run it off.'

But I had to go off in the 89th minute, and when I had a scan, they told me I had done the cruciate ligament and it would need surgery. 'No chance,' I said, and rejected it out of hand.

I had an MRI scan and was sent to two cruciate-injuries specialists in the north of England. I was told the cruciate ligament prevents the knee giving way when bent or changing direction and helps to provide stability and balance – which makes it even more vital for a footballer. Players like Paul Gascoigne, Ruud van Nistelrooy, Robert Pires and Alan Shearer had all been to the same specialists and undergone surgery because it guarantees full recovery – but it means weeks out of the game. I reported the specialists' advice back to Ibrox

A boy on a beach: we may have been poor, but life was good in Trinidad, my Caribbean paradise island

At home with my dad and little brother Micah. We missed Dad when he had to go away to find work

The Big Day: Micah and I opening our Christmas presents

Fun in the backyard with Micah and our cousin

Lunch at our grandmother's home: I couldn't stop eating to look at the camera

The Zion Praise Centre in Kirkcaldy is the centre of my spiritual world. I read the Bible daily, lead prayers and preach

One of the greatest days of my life: 16 March 2004, when Livingston beat Hibs 2–0 in the CIS Cup final at Hampden

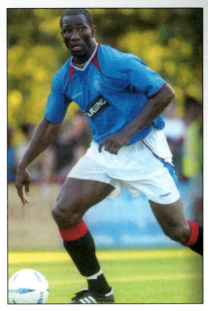

One of my first appearances in a Rangers jersey in a pre-season game in Austria in 2004

I scored one of the best goals of my career for Livingston against Dundee United in the 2002–03 season – and my sweatshirt says it all

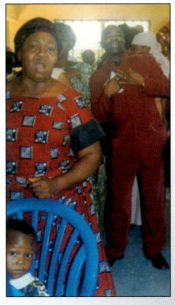

Pastor Joe Nwokoye, my spiritual mentor, dancing with his congregation in Nigeria

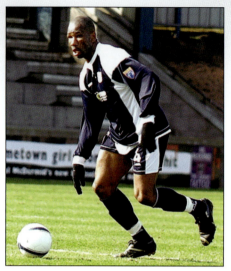

Home again: back in a Raith Rovers strip for the 2006–07 season (Photograph © Tony Fimister)

Deal done: with Gordon Brown, lifelong Raith Rovers fan and MP for Kirkcaldy, and Raith Rovers manager Craig Levein at the Zion Praise Centre, when we agreed that I would return to my first Scottish club

– but I still said that God would heal my knee. As before, with my shoulder injury, I spoke to Pastor Joe about my decision not to have the surgery and he prayed with me. I decided to rely on the word of God.

That was when it hit the headlines, and I found I had the most famous knee in Britain! It was one of the most talked-about injuries of all time. People were stopping me in the street and asking me if I really believed that God would heal me.

I still have a copy of the letter sent on 21 March 2005 by Mr Paul J. Rae of Manchester, the eminent consultant orthopaedic surgeon and specialist in reconstructive knee surgery. It shows the punishment a footballer's legs take in normal playing and training. It also confirms that I suffered a 'significant' injury, advises against playing or training, and recommends waiting for nearly two months before surgery. I was left in no doubt by the surgeon and the medical team at Ibrox that, if I did not have the operation, my footballing days were numbered.

Mr Rae's letter to Rangers said:

> As you know, he injured his left knee when he suffered a probable hyperextension injury when he was involved in a tackle with another player and struck the back of the opponent's leg.
>
> There was some question about an earlier incident when his left knee seemed to buckle slightly and also an injury previously which did produce some postero-lateral pain but responded well to physio input. With his recent injury, there was immediate posterial and postero-lateral pain and he was brought off immediately.

He refers to the MRI scans I had and notes, 'There is a past history of medial ligament injury to both knees, which kept him out for about six weeks, but he reports no problems since then.'

Those scans confirmed 'acute injury to the anterior cruciate ligament', and Mr Rae declares, 'I think this is a significant injury, and I would advise against trying to play or train. I would advise bracing to allow the posterior capsule to heal and then I would plan a left anterior cruciate ligament reconstruction in approximately 6–8 weeks from his injury, providing the knee has settled down satisfactorily.'

Knowing my resistance to surgery, his last word to Rangers was: 'Ultimately, the decision does rest with Marvin, but I think it should be emphasised there is a risk of severely aggravating the knee and making the situation worse.'

I respect the medical profession for the wonderful work that they do, and I am not against operations. I know doctors and surgeons are there to help you, because God has blessed them with that ability. They do a fantastic job saving lives and mending bodies. But I saw it differently. I thought, 'God created that knee, so why can't he fix it?' You might yet see me go under the knife, but only if it is the will of God. As long as it is the will of God, it will be OK with me.

It was no coincidence that my return was against Celtic at Ibrox on 24 April 2005. I had not played for six weeks, not even reserve games – just one bounce game on the training ground to make sure I was moving in the way I had done before the injury. It was a gamble for Alex McLeish, and it showed how much the all-important Old Firm games had come to depend on one-on-one battles between big men on either side. The papers were saying that Rangers needed me because of the physical presence of the Celtic team, while others were warning that I could break down at any time. It was said that my presence would be missed at the set pieces.

Within myself, I knew I had come through the tough tests of the physio and training sessions, which involved one-on-one work and a lot of twisting and turning, but the manager pointed out that you cannot simulate match conditions – especially the competitiveness of a game against Celtic – in training.

The pressure was unbelievable, not only on me but also on the manager, because he was the one who had to select the team for one of the most critical games in the club's history. When we were still two points behind Celtic so late in the season, everyone said we needed to win that game against them to have any chance of the League championship. It was bound to be a hard, physical encounter, and if we lost, the fans would be saying, 'You should never have played Marvin.' Playing me would decide my future one way or the other – but it meant Alex McLeish taking a big risk that could lose the Premier League title and, perhaps, his job. He said at the time, 'The point is, if I continue not to pick him, this could go on till the end of his contract. So I'll probably have to play him to find out. That means waiting for something to happen, or not to happen, and that way convince either me or him.'

Right up to the 12.30 p.m. kick-off, everyone was kept in the dark, partly to keep Celtic guessing, but mainly because Alex McLeish had genuinely not made up his mind. It was not until the supporters saw me warming up with my teammates that they knew I was playing again.

My knee was really tested in the first minutes when Craig Bellamy charged into our penalty area chasing a through ball and both the goalie, Ronald Waterreus, and I threw ourselves at it. When we collided, you could hear the sharp intake of breath all round Ibrox, but I jumped straight back onto my feet to show there were no ill effects.

We lost an early goal when Petrov scored. I was close to him and I knew I could have done better to stop that goal. It was not really the result of the injury but the fact that I was a bit rusty and my timing was slightly off from being out of first-team play for so long.

We were 2–0 down at half-time, and, although we dug deep and played our hearts out, nothing whatsoever was happening for us. I still managed to show what I could do when I had a header come off the Celtic crossbar. If that had gone in, we would have shared the points, because Stevie Thompson scored our only goal with two minutes left.

I was substituted in the 83rd minute, although everybody said I had played well. Despite having no surgery, then, my knee had held out. I have been told I am fortunate that my quad muscles surrounding the knee are so powerful that they allowed me to overcome the cruciate injury. That may be the way the medical men and the physios explain it, but, of course, it was God who gave me those muscles . . .

Celtic's 2–1 win left them five points ahead with four matches to play, and the 'experts' said it showed their superiority over us. Although it now seemed hopeless, I kept telling my teammates and the fans to keep believing because we were still going to win the league. That was when players started coming up to me to ask

'Will God help us?' I told them that they would see.

A 3–1 win at Aberdeen kept us within two points, but the match will be remembered for bringing disgrace on Scottish football. For some reason, games between Rangers and Aberdeen have always brought out the worst in their fans, and this time they went too far.

At the home supporters' end, there was a hail of cartons, cups and other objects every time a Rangers player went near. Our captain Fernando Ricksen was singled out for special treatment, probably because he is such a dangerous player, and a woman was arrested for spitting on him, while referee Hugh Dallas was struck by a plastic bottle when he went to deal with it.

That was disgusting enough, but it became dangerous when Fernando was hit by a coin as he was getting ready to take a corner. Earlier in the season, he'd needed a stitch in his head after being hit by a coin at Celtic Park. We all agreed with Fernando when he spoke out after the match and appealed to the football and police authorities to take stronger action because this type of behaviour was ruining the game. Players are disciplined for doing anything that inflames the fans, and there should be the same discipline in the crowd.

The match was almost called off at half-time when torrential rain left puddles of water all over the pitch and Alex McLeish told the officials it needed to be drained if play was to go on. The conditions were a searching test of my knee, and the Aberdeen manager Jimmy Calderwood picked out Dado Prso and me as being standouts for Rangers.

Alex McLeish commented that I was looking much sharper, although he still had his doubts about my refusal to have surgery: 'He could go the rest of his career without needing surgery. It's happened before. We have good medical people who are quite perturbed, but it's Marvin's choice.'

The fans had certainly got the message about the power of faith, because at our next home game against Hearts there was a big banner in one of the stands that said 'Keep believing'. I have to say I really tested their faith, because I was both hero and villain in that game! The 'Marvin's Miracle' headlines came out again because I scored just before half-time, to add to an early goal by Thomas Buffel and sew up the game. Late in the match, however, I stuck out my boot to turn away a free-kick – and deflected it into the corner of our own net! These things happen when you are desperate to get the ball out of the danger area. It made for an anxious last ten minutes, but we held on for a 2–1 win.

Sunday, 22 May 2005, the last day of the season, was an absolutely amazing day for Scottish football. We had chased Celtic down to the finishing line, but they only had to beat Motherwell to make the championship theirs – again! We knew we had to beat Hibs on their home ground to have any chance, and we were determined to go all out just in case there was a surprise at Fir Park, although it did not seem possible that Celtic would let it slip away from them.

The whole day had a mixed atmosphere. I thought it was a perfect stage for God to do a miracle, but in the morning in the hotel everybody was subdued. There was doubt in their minds, and they were worried. We could win the game against Hibs, but it was all about what Celtic and Motherwell would do. There was a lot of negativity, and the Rangers fans seemed to be harbouring the same doubts, because there was not the usual number of them at Easter Road, only the really loyal followers.

We heard a big cheer from the Hibs fans. Chris Sutton had scored an early goal for Celtic, and they were singing against us.

After Nacho Novo scored for us, we were playing a holding game, passing and passing. With two minutes remaining on the clock, Celtic were leading 1–0, and the title seemed to be signed, sealed and delivered to Parkhead. Then we heard a big cheer from the Rangers fans. Scott MacDonald had scored for Motherwell to make it 1–1, and we began to think, 'It's really, really happening.' I was thanking God and just praying we would not make any mistakes at the back.

The atmosphere became unreal, because if we kept it at 1–0, we could win the championship, and Hibs just needed Aberdeen not to score in their game to qualify for the UEFA Cup. We were taking no chances and playing the game in the corners of the field when an even bigger cheer went up because MacDonald had scored yet again. I just said, 'Lord Almighty, you are so wonderful!'

When the final whistle went, the championship was ours. I fell on my knees in the middle of the park and raised my arms to the heavens. One fan ran on and hugged me and actually started crying. He said, 'I just love you so much, man – I believe, I believe!' All the Rangers fans invaded the pitch, and it was just crazy. People were dumbfounded.

It was one of the greatest days of my life – to have won the championship in the space of just two minutes showed that if you keep believing in God to the very end, He will never disappoint you. That is just what I did: I held on to God to the end and He gave me my reward for my belief and my trust.

After 38 games, it had come down to a single point – 93 to 92 – and we had won the title thanks to a shock win by Motherwell, the team we had beaten 4–1 the previous week.

The manager came into the dressing-room and said, 'Marv, you are actually a god now at Ibrox!' I just laughed because, at the end of a season in which miracle after miracle had been performed, I was still wearing the T-shirt that I always wear saying 'With God Nothing Is Impossible'.

Beside the drama of the League championship, Rangers' other achievements in the 2004–05 season are easily forgotten. We won the CIS Cup and reached the group stage of the UEFA Cup, although we were knocked out of the Scottish Cup in the third round.

The scores in the last two games of the CIS tournament showed the real Rangers: 7–1 over Dundee United in the semi-final and 5–1 over Motherwell in the final. When I was out of action, I missed playing in the final – I would have been the first player to take part in back-to-back finals for different winning teams.

We just failed to make the group stage of the Champions League. I was on the subs' bench when we lost the first leg of the qualifier against CSKA Moscow 2–1. It was a 1–1 draw in the return leg at Ibrox, and I was sent on for the last ten minutes to act as an auxiliary forward, but we could not force the match into extra-time, and that single-goal deficit on the 3–2 aggregate meant Rangers lost out on an estimated potential windfall of about £8 million.

There were so many good players and good friends at Ibrox, and some made a strong impression on me – none more so than Barry Ferguson, as a player, a person and an inspirational team leader.

What I got from Barry is that he is a winner. He hates losing, even at training games or playing pool with the guys. He was told he would never make it in football and has proved everybody wrong. It was his dream that he would play for Rangers and Scotland, and he fulfilled that through his talent and sheer determination.

Given all these things and knowing he was an icon in Scotland, when I met him I would not have been surprised if there had been arrogance in his manner, but he is one of the nicest men you could ever meet. He is also a caring person when you really get to know him, and I respected him even more when he went out of his way to tell me that he respected my beliefs.

Among my other teammates, Dado Prso was fantastic, Alex Rae was so solid to play behind and Gregory Vignal was simply outstanding in defence or midfield – it was a pity that terms could not be agreed when Rangers wanted to sign him on a permanent contract. Guys like Craig Moore, Mikel Arteta and Nacho Novo, goalkeepers Ronald Waterreus and Stefan Klos, and younger players such as Chris Burke, Alan Hutton, Kris Boyd and Stevie Smith all made playing for that Rangers team an exceptional experience.

Dado, as well as being an outstanding player, is also one of the greatest guys ever. He is Croatian, and Croatians seem to like to dress up with a special style. He often took a ribbing in the changing-room because his dress sense is so . . . well, different. He is always proud of what he is wearing, and I like people like that. He is so happy with who he is and revels in the fact that people get enjoyment out of his clothes, because they are laughing with him and not at him. Dado is just a fun guy, but when he is on the field he is the most serious professional.

It was such a good bunch of players, along with the rest of the staff, from the chairman David Murray through the management, the cleaners, the medical and the technical staff – like Hendo the physio, who was a really good friend, the doctor Ian McGuinnes, and Jimmy Bell the kit-man, who was so funny and had been there for years – that I used to look forward to going to work.

The season ended on a very moving note for me when I was voted the Rangers Players' Player of the Year. At the presentation dinner, I was given the biggest cheer of the night and a standing ovation from my teammates and the club supporters.

It was a great honour for me, because it was my teammates who had voted among themselves and chosen me when there were so many great players, such as Dado Prso, Nacho Novo and Fernando Ricksen, who had all been top guns for Rangers that season.

I could not help recalling that a lot of people didn't think I could succeed at Ibrox, and I'd had to earn the right to play in the Rangers first-team. I always stayed positive and told myself I could play at that level. That award showed I had done a good job for Rangers.

Rangers' 2005–06 season was very different, with poor performances in the domestic competitions at home. Our performance in the SPL was so below par – for Rangers, that is – that it caused a complete upheaval at the club and the eventual departure of Alex McLeish.

Completely overlooked and almost forgotten in that

season is that we created another piece of history by becoming the first-ever Scottish club to qualify for the last 16 of the Champions League, although Celtic managed it later. To be up there among the most prestigious teams in Europe, if not the world, should count for something!

It is a strange thing that a manager can pull off such a coup, with all that it means in leadership and tactical guile, and yet be judged a 'failure'. If you are the man in charge at Ibrox, though, what really matters is the comparison with Celtic and whoever is on top in Scotland.

That does not explain why Rangers, after the triumph of the previous season, should have gone into such a slump so soon. We were largely the same team, with the same talent and character, the same manager and coaches and the same incentives to repeat our success. So what made the difference?

I put it down to the fact that we did not appreciate what God had done the season before. It is like being ungrateful when someone does something for you. If you do not show your gratitude, then when you come back and ask them to do the same again, they will not do it. That is how God is: He does something for you, but if you do not appreciate it, you cannot expect Him to do it for you again. What happened is that we never acknowledged God's gift to us, and that is why the season that followed was a very up-and-down one. I was the only person at Rangers who came out and said the Lord had given us that championship. Nobody else appreciated that God had performed a miracle for the club. If people at Rangers had only shown their appreciation of God's goodness to them, no one would have been able to stop Rangers in the following season.

The grace of God was still there, as shown by our reaching the last 16 in the Champions League. That is something that can never be taken away from Rangers FC or the squad of players at that particular time. We played some good games in the Champions League, but we did it the hard way, picking up points from the two great teams who were favourites to go through: Porto and Inter Milan. In the group stage, we were beaten only once – by Inter Milan – and we picked up a very important point away from home against Porto. I had been on the subs' bench for earlier games, but Alex McLeish shook things up for the game in Portugal. Most of the game, we were holding off heavy pressure from a very lively Porto attack, who fired in cleverly angled balls and sent over dangerous crosses from out wide. It was our two young substitutes who won the all-important point for us – Chris Burke headed into the path of 19-year-old Ross McCormack, who slipped the ball into the net.

The surprise team in our group was Bratislava. We thought we would pick up maximum points against them, but we drew twice and just could not seem to beat them.

We qualified for the last 16 thanks to a 1–1 draw against Inter Milan at Ibrox in December 2005. Rangers were playing under a shadow because of our poor domestic results, and there was a lot of speculation that it might actually be Alex McLeish's last game in charge. In contrast, Inter were at the top of Serie A, and they had seasoned World Cup players such as their captain Marco Materazzi, who was a general on field and always a danger at set pieces. We were also up against players such as Adriano, an amazing striker, and Martins, who has electrifying pace – and both were absolutely on fire that season, scoring goals for fun.

THE RANGERS MIRACLE

It did not take long for me to realise I was up against two of the best strikers in the world. After half an hour, Mihajlovic swung in a ball that just seemed to hang in the air and Adriano rose through a ruck of players to nod it into the net. After that, I was determined to give nothing else away – perhaps that is why I was given the yellow card – and I had a really good game. Peter Lovenkrands, playing up front for most of the game as a lone striker, was our goal-scoring hero.

We had an anxious wait for the final score from Bratislava, and when we heard Artmedia and Porto had drawn 0–0, we knew our point against Inter was enough to get us through. Once again, Rangers fans who had stayed behind were celebrating not just our performance but also the result from another ground.

The higher we went in Europe, the more obvious it was that the cuts and the financial tightening which had taken place at Ibrox were having an effect. Rangers' big-spending ways, which had bought success in the past, could not have continued. Alex McLeish was clearly unhappy that, even after the league and CIS Cup Double win, he was forced to downsize the squad and rely on inexperienced players and free transfers. In the Champions League, we were up against top clubs with big money to spend on quality players.

Rangers have been built on success, success, success. Fans and the media did not want to think about the real reasons for the slump and did not give Alex credit for what he did with the resources at his command, nor for the fact that he took three clubs he has managed into Europe.

When Rangers came up against the Spanish side Villarreal in the last 16, we were regarded as the underdogs, with no chance of reaching the quarter-finals. But there were times when we made them look like the outsiders, and they only edged through on away goals. After a 2–2 draw at Ibrox, the boys played their hearts out and it finished 1–1 in Spain, leaving Villarreal with their vital additional away goal.

Alex McLeish was under intense pressure because everyone knew that Rangers' exit from the Champions League meant he would be making his own exit from Ibrox. That performance, which I watched from the subs' bench, meant he could walk away with his head held high. In a very emotional speech, he said his strongest feeling at that moment was not disappointment but extreme pride in the players and everybody else connected with such a fantastic performance.

This was set against the poor start to the domestic season and our defence of the SPL championship, winning only six league games out of the first seventeen – but worse was to come.

While we were performing heroics in the Champions League from October through to early December, we had the worst run in the club's history – ten games without a win. We got only as far as the quarter-finals of the CIS Cup, and when Hibs beat us 3–1 in the fourth round of the Scottish Cup (their third win over Rangers in the season), that ended our last realistic chance of winning any silverware.

Then, just as suddenly as it had all gone wrong, we had a complete change of fortune. A major reason for this was the signing from Kilmarnock of Kris Boyd, an amazing young talent who was already the SPL's top scorer. Kris made a dream start, with seven goals in his first four games in Rangers blue – and the club was off on a 16-match unbeaten run.

In his fourth match, Kris got two against Inverness CT, and I got on the scoresheet by diving between two defenders and forcing the ball over the line. I will admit that it went in off my shoulder, but they all count, especially when your team is coming out of a slump.

It was a very strange and unsettling time for the players. From the turn of the year, we all knew we were playing for a manager who would be leaving us – yet we still wanted to do our best for him. In fact, we got word that a big announcement would be made after the last of our group matches in the Champions League. But our success in coming out of that group with a place in the last 16 changed that. It would obviously have been unfair, even foolish, to sack a manager at such a time of triumph. Instead, chairman David Murray stated that Alex McLeish would remain in charge indefinitely, although the SPL results would need to improve.

Everybody was jittery and uncertain and also feeling the strain of the European campaign. When we tumbled out of the Scottish Cup, then lost 2–0 to Aberdeen, there were demonstrations by fans against the manager and the chairman. The newspapers were full of stories that David Murray would let Alex McLeish go. They even named his successor: Paul Le Guen, the former Lyon coach, who had been having secret talks about the job.

In February 2006, it was announced that the manager would be leaving at the end of the season. It was just two days before the crucial Old Firm match at Ibrox – which, not surprisingly, we lost 1–0. The result put Gordon Strachan's team completely out of sight at the top of the table on 56 points, an uncatchable 18 points ahead of Rangers. We were scrapping with Aberdeen and Hearts for second place and the chance of European football the following season. One writer even suggested that, with more than three months to go, Celtic could go on holiday and wait for an official letter confirming them as SPL champions!

For the Rangers players, and probably the fans, the rest of the season was unreal. We were working just as hard, training and going into every match with the same will to win. With Celtic completely out of sight at number one, we kept up the pressure on Hearts for that second place, with Europe as the real prize.

Alex McLeish told us he was going to give Rangers 100 per cent right up to the last game and he expected the same of us. No one could have any doubts about our commitment as we clawed our way back to within a single point of Hearts.

We were still in third place when we went to Kilmarnock on 29 April, and I had one of the games of my life. I was on the bench at the start, as I had been for a few weeks, but Alex McLeish sent me on at half-time after Kilmarnock got an early goal – and I got a double.

Alex was still putting everything into his job, as anyone would have realised if they had been listening at the dressing-room door! He gave the team a real roasting for being one down when we were desperate for every point; in fact, when a reporter asked Stevie Smith what the manager had said to make such a difference, Stevie said tactfully that the boss's remarks had been 'ungentlemanly' . . .

Just after I got on the park, I got the equalising goal from a free-kick by Stevie. Kris Boyd put us ahead against his old club, and I finished it off when I got my head onto a long cross from Chris Burke.

One newspaper headline read 'Marvin The Marvellous'.

It is expected for a forward to come off the bench and score two goals, but I am a defender. That sort of thing is not supposed to happen, but my career has been full of unlikely events.

We did not realise it at the time, but that same weekend the result that did the damage to Rangers' European hopes happened at Tynecastle: Hearts 3 Celtic 0. It was Hearts' first victory over Celtic that season, and it was perfectly timed. They badly needed the points because Rangers had closed to within a point of them. Celtic did not need points because they had sewn up the championship a month earlier when they beat Hearts 1–0. What made it even more galling was the report that both sets of supporters, who had been slagging each other the rest of the afternoon, were united in singing 'Let's all laugh at Rangers'.

Hearts tied up the second place with a midweek win over Aberdeen. It was a bitter disappointment, but when Hearts came to Ibrox for the last game of the season – and Alex McLeish's last match with Rangers – the occasion was more bitter than it should have been. We easily beat them 2–0, thanks to two more goals from Kris Boyd (bringing his total for the season to an amazing 37, of which 20 were scored during his short time with Rangers), but there was no joy in it. Their manager, Valdas Ivanauskas, made nine changes and brought on a number of complete unknowns. No doubt he had the forthcoming Scottish Cup final in mind, but the Rangers supporters took it as an insult, and the atmosphere became even more sour when the Hearts fans sang 'We're only here for the party'.

On the field, we were determined to show that, whatever game Hearts might be playing, we would be thoroughly professional to the end and give our fans a last hurrah. At the end, Alex McLeish came onto the pitch to make his farewells. The players stayed on the pitch as well – we knew that a number of us would also be saying goodbye to Ibrox . . .

It was really a shame about Alex McLeish. For one thing, he did not get full credit for what he had done for Rangers, winning two championships and five trophies in five years. All the players appreciated him as the boss, and we felt we let him down in that last season because our performance just did not match the standard and capabilities we had shown in the previous season. In the last games under Alex, we were determined to give our all for him, to do our best for the man who had given us so much and to wish him the best for the future. Alex did well for me, stood up for me against criticism and did his best for the club and the players.

When I first went to Motherwell, a raw young player from Trinidad, Alex was quite right to say that he was looking for a defender with experience of the Scottish game. I didn't have a clue about the Scottish game, so I respected his decision and moved on from there. At that stage in my development, I was too green and would probably have flopped in the SPL, but when he signed me for Rangers I was prepared, mentally stronger, wiser, knew more about the game and just fitted in.

From then on, we had a good relationship, because he knew there was no malice and I always take rejection as a good thing. I knew he had nothing against me, in fact quite the opposite – which he proved time and time again when I was at Rangers.

Strangely, it was right at the end of his Rangers managership that I most admired him. Everybody knew he was going and would have understood if he had not given complete commitment in the closing games, but he kept battling to the very end, showing real strength of character and his determination to do the right thing.

Whatever his critics may have said about Alex, he made an honourable exit and was able to leave Ibrox with his head held high. That is why he will always be treated with respect by anyone who cares about the game of football.

I always believe that everything happens for a reason, and I was not in the least surprised when, after leaving Rangers, Alex became Scotland's manager.

When Paul Le Guen took over at Ibrox, I had a rough idea that I would be one of those who would be leaving, because that is the way it works with a new manager. It had been announced that he would have a war chest with which to strengthen the squad, thanks to a £48-million tie-up with JJB Sports in a ten-year deal with an initial, up-front payment of £18 million that June. It was obvious he would be importing new players, although it was startling that he brought in at least ten, and there would be a big clear-out in the close season. As a footballer, you respect the fact that everybody has different views. One manager might like me, but another might not think my style of play fits in with his ideas for the team. Alex McLeish had hired me with a specific role in mind. Paul Le Guen had different plans, and I was not part of them. You have to respect a manager's decision, and I respected him for telling me upfront and not trying to play me along. He called me in and said I would be given a free transfer because I did not feature in his plans for the coming season.

A lot of people told me they regretted it because of

the relationships I had built at the club; they said they would miss the fun and the chat and the talking about God. For me, it was the end of a chapter. I also believed that it must have meant God did not want me at Rangers Football Club anymore and that it was time for me to move on.

From the very start of the Le Guen managership, the results were bad and not what everyone had expected from the change of regime. It was said in the papers and on websites that perhaps things might have been different if I and a few others had still been there. When I moved back to Raith Rovers, my first Scottish club, they had my complete loyalty, but I still wished Rangers well and felt for them in their troubles.

Within a few weeks, they were trailing well behind Celtic, and I was refusing to comment on the reasons because my focus was on my own club. Even so, I was absolutely astonished by the sensation that followed. When Paul Le Guen stripped Barry Ferguson of the captaincy and almost forced him to leave Ibrox, it was an astonishing blunder for a manager to make.

Barry and I were constantly on the phone to each other, so we were in close touch throughout the episode. I know how deeply it hurt him and how it caused him unnecessary personal turmoil.

Although Le Guen had told me I had no place in his plans, I was prepared to respect him and wished him well. But his handling of the Barry Ferguson affair showed he had no understanding of the player or the club.

Rangers FC have had many great players, great captains and great servants. Barry Ferguson is up there with the most commanding, the most committed and the most loyal. I was not surprised when the reaction of the fans and the club was one of outrage. I knew immediately that, if it came to a straight choice between Le Guen and Barry, there would only be one winner. The fans would have created mayhem if Barry had gone. They would have been right, because it would have been grossly unfair – and suicide for Rangers FC.

Chapter Five

SOCA WARRIOR

The T&T international team are known as the 'Soca Warriors' and our women's team are the 'Soca Princesses'. Many people think this is from 'soccer', but 'Soca' is the Trinidadian dance music that evolved from calypso – and that just about sums up our attitude to the beautiful game.

We all know the old Bill Shankly saying that football is more important than life and death. We take it seriously in T&T – but it also has to be *fun*. Anybody who experienced the carnival atmosphere surrounding our World Cup games in Germany in 2006 would know that.

All of our international players are known to the T&T fans by nicknames that sum up each individual's style of play. Russell Latapy is 'Latas' or 'The Little Magician', one of our midfielders is Kerwyn 'Hardest' Jemmott and our top-scoring World Cup striker Anthony Wolfe is 'Howling Wolfe'. Wrexham's Dennis Lawrence and I in the backline were known as the 'Twin Towers'.

My other nickname back home is 'Dog'; off the field, they call me 'The Gentle Giant', but on the field they call me Dog. It was given to me when I was about 13 because a guy saw me getting frenetic, winding myself up and running about the field. He said, 'You're acting like a dog!' and from that day it stuck. If you look me up on the Internet, you'll see that to this day they call me Marvin 'Dog' Andrews, because they think I play like a Rottweiler!

T&T players have started to spread out across the football world, and you will find them in the English Premiership, Europe, the US, Japan, Africa, Australia and many other countries. And there are many more unknowns back home who could hold their own wherever they go.

I believe the talented players in Trinidad and Tobago have not been marketed properly and, with no one to take them to the higher level, they have not been as fortunate as me. When they reach a certain level and a certain age and do not see a future, they turn to drugs or get caught up in the other temptations that are waiting for young people. I hope that our qualifying for the 2006 World Cup has done something to change that.

Scotland was one of the first countries to latch on to the talent that there has always been in Trinidad and Tobago. Over the years, Soca Warriors like Tony Rougier, Jerren Nixon, Lyndon Andrews, Collin Samuel, Russell Latapy, Jason Scotland, Arnold Dwarika and Brent Sancho have all played for Scottish clubs.

As I have described, when he was manager at Dundee United, Ian McCall – who is a very good judge – had a number of my countrymen on his books and made a bid for me when I was at Livingston. To begin with, the attraction was that our good players were available for not much money – a big factor for cash-strapped Scottish clubs – but Ian McCall said publicly that he admired the way T&T produced guys who are two-footed, have a bit of flair and are naturally strong.

In the same city, when Jim Duffy was manager of Dundee United, he took his team to Trinidad to get match practice against our local clubs and came back reporting that he had seen three or four players who could make an immediate jump into the SPL. He said, 'The language isn't a problem and I like the fact that they all tend to play the game with a smile on their faces.'

I played my own game as a defender, relying on my strength and my attributes in the air, and I always wanted to get up for the set pieces and get on the scoresheet. The one thing all my managers and coaches have singled out for comment is my attitude – and that is pure Trinidad!

Russell Latapy is one of the most talented players I've ever seen or played with, although it is said that one of his brothers was even better but didn't apply himself in the same way. Russell is simply the total footballer and a brilliant ball-player with flair and skill. He may not be as aggressive as, say, the Roy Keane type of hard-driving midfield player or a Steven Gerrard, because he does not have the same engine these guys have, but every time he has the ball you can expect something special from him, just as you can from Ronaldinho. Sometimes Russell seems so laid-back, but every time he has the ball at his feet there seems to be a silence as everybody waits for him to do something magical – hence his nickname. He is so small, yet makes the game of football look so easy against much bigger players. He also keeps himself super-fit and looks set to go on forever, especially in his new role as player–coach.

Dwight Yorke is another outstandingly talented player, fantastically strong and skilful. Despite striking ability and his consistent marksmanship, he played midfield throughout the World Cup qualifiers. The manager knew that Dwight could tackle and defend as well as be the midfield tactician. Russell didn't have the defensive mentality nor the inclination to get back. Dwight could sit back, and Russell was given the licence to roam and cause trouble anywhere in the 40 yards from the opposition goal. He can cause trouble for defences, win a free-kick or penalty and create a goal out of nothing.

T&T football is not as fast as the Scottish or British game. The 100 mph game is not in the Trinidadian culture, so the pace is much slower; we pass and pass. The Caribbean game is about skill, and in the attacking third of the pitch you will see players do amazing tricks. There was actually a spell a few years ago when our national team was rated higher than Scotland! In fairness, I do have to admit that in May 2004 we were beaten 4–1 by Bertie Vogts's Scotland in a friendly at Easter Road.

Playing in my late teens in Caribbean Cup and invitational tournaments, we came up against teams such as Mexico, Puerto Rico, Costa Rica and Colombia. It was always being said that Trinidadians were laid-back, but these teams taught us a lesson about aggressiveness. They demonstrated a lot of skill and quick-wittedness, but there were also times when they were too vicious, and our team was subjected to rough play, spitting and other forms of gamesmanship.

I am approaching my century of caps for my country, and I hope to have many more. My first goal at senior international level was on 4 March 2000, in a 5–0 win over Antilles in a World Cup qualifier.

Qualifying for the World Cup finals was something the

country had been craving for years. T&T came very close to making it to the 1974 and 1990 finals; we were cheated out of the former, and the final qualifier for the 1990 finals was such a freak result that the disappointment caused a tremendous setback to the game in Trinidad.

In December 1973, there was outrage when we were clearly robbed against Haiti. Our group's qualifying matches were played in Haiti, and the record will show that T&T finished second to the hosts and had the best goal difference in the group. It is said that the 1973 team was the best-ever squad to wear our country's colours. The fact that we had handed out a 4–0 drubbing to Mexico showed the quality of that T&T team, which would have been on the plane to Germany had they managed to draw or beat Haiti. The scoreline on 4 December 1973 was Haiti 2 T&T 1. But behind that result lies what everyone in football now admits was one of the most outrageous scandals in the history of the World Cup.

After 15 minutes, the teams had a goal each – then began a series of very strange decisions. T&T went into the lead with a goal that was given by the ref, and the teams were ready to restart, but, after consulting the linesman, he reversed his decision because it was claimed there had been a foul on the Haitian goalkeeper. At 30 minutes, a T&T goal scored when a long throw-in was deflected into the net was chalked off for some inexplicable reason. Before half-time, another T&T goal was ruled offside and a fourth at 61 minutes. All the play and all the pressure had been ours, and we hit the post once, but Haiti got a second goal two minutes from time. The referee allowed the game to go the full 90 minutes, but it was clear that our team had no chance of ever winning that match.

After the game, T&T lodged an official complaint with FIFA, and the referee, Salvadoran Jose Enrique, and linesman, James Higuet of Canada, were both banned for life – the most drastic punishment they could hand out. After that, simple justice should have meant that, at the very least, the game was replayed, but, although there must have been very serious justification for the verdicts on the referee and linesman, the result was allowed to stand.

It was one of the great injustices of football, and it still rankles in my home country. No team gets so many goals disallowed, and our entire nation felt the game should have been replayed on neutral territory.

All I will say is that the match was played in Haiti's capital, Port-au-Prince, in the dark days of 'Papa Doc' Duvalier's dictatorship and the terrifying 'Tonton Macoutes', when many strange things happened . . .

It was no consolation to Trinidad that Haiti's so-called 'triumph' ended in disgrace in the finals in Germany when their defender Ernst Jean-Joseph became the first World Cup player ever to fail a dope test. It was typical of what happened in Haiti in those days that Jean-Joseph was dragged back to the training camp, held against his will and beaten up by his own officials.

Qualification for the 1990 finals in Italy was also within T&T's grasp, but, after coming so tantalisingly close to our World Cup dream, it was again snatched away – this time by a freak goal.

On 19 November 1989, one point from a draw in the last qualifying match against the USA on our home ground in Port of Spain would have sent us to Italy. As far as we were concerned, our team – known in those days as the 'Strike Squad' – were already on their way.

At the time I was 13, and I remember the whole country was in red. The game was a sell-out (the estimated attendance that day was around 50,000, in a stadium where the official capacity was 32,000). People were viewing TV sets in shop windows, and I watched the match wearing my national colours. It turned out to be a day we would never forget – for the wrong reason!

We were left weeping in disbelief when a tame, speculative shot by the USA's Paul Caligiuri from 40 yards somehow found the net for the only goal of the game and the Americans made the trip to the finals. It became known as 'the shot heard round the world'.

After that, the country went into a real low. It was such a deep disappointment that everybody seemed to turn against the sport, and it set football in T&T back a long way. The result haunted us for years – and from that day, when I was just a teenager, I said in my heart, 'I want to be part of the team that takes my country to the World Cup.'

I was fortunate to come under the influence of two great coaches: Keith LokLoy and Bertille St Clair. Keith LokLoy, the former national youth coach who became FIFA's development officer, took me into the Under-20 national team at 17. He instilled in his players aggression and a belief that they could make it. He did just that for me and was such an inspiration. Bertille St Clair, our former national coach, was the same type of manager. He had me working so hard and instilled the notion in us that nothing comes good without hard work and the desire to win – but most of all plain, old-fashioned hard work.

Dwight Yorke was Bertille's protégé. He has his own football academy, and Dwight was in it from the age of six!

When Aston Villa toured in Trinidad, they spotted him, and he had trials with them at 17. When Dwight moved to Manchester United, Bertille recalled, 'I got £12,000 for Dwight Yorke, whilst Villa got £12 million! But money wasn't a problem – all I wanted was to get the young man out there.'

Following a leg break which prematurely ended his playing career at 17, and still makes him limp today, Bertille started teaching PE, first at primary and then at secondary level, with the Signal Hill school in Tobago. He also started the St Clair academy in 1976, which now coaches more than 200 children from age six upwards. His success with both – the academy has won four Tobago League titles whilst the college side has won seven inter-collegiate titles since 1981 – eventually led to his appointment as national team coach, and he remains a great influence in Caribbean football.

I've been under different managers who have all improved my game, but these two from an early age helped me to develop a mental toughness and the knowledge that I could make it if I applied myself.

I won my first full international cap in January 1996, just after I had turned 20. Over the years, the T&T managership kept changing drastically, and I have actually lost count of the head coaches in my time, although I know it is at least ten!

Things changed for the better when Ian Porterfield was signed in the hope of at last getting us into the World Cup finals. Under him, we were described as dominating Caribbean soccer, and he took us to our eighth win in the Copa Caribe championships. When he came to T&T, he was already a vastly experienced manager and coach at club and international level. Coincidentally, he was born in Fife, where I began my Scottish football, and he played for Raith Rovers, the club that has played such a large part in my life.

He had been in charge at Sheffield United, Aberdeen, Reading and Chelsea and had coached developing countries such as Zambia, Saudi Arabia, Zimbabwe and Oman. Since leaving T&T, he has worked in Korea and Armenia – if ever a man spread the football gospel, it is Ian Porterfield!

I managed to score in his first two qualifying games against Netherlands Antilles, one amongst the many in an emphatic 5–0 victory at home and the winner in a 1–0 away win. I was delighted that I was described as being 'a tower of strength' in defence but was also noted for coming forward and scoring goals when we needed them.

The truth is, I was alongside some outstanding players, but they remained unknown in the wider football world because they preferred to stay on in Trinidad and play in Caribbean tournaments.

In the full international side for World Cup qualifying matches, we were able to call on players such as Russell Latapy, Dwight Yorke, Tony Rougier, Stern John, who was then playing for Nottingham Forest, and Shaka Hislop – all flair players, but I wanted to go back home and have people say, 'Marvin Andrews is the best defender we have produced.'

Before the 2002 Japan/South Korea finals – which everybody believed we would reach – we were placed 29th in the FIFA world rankings after victories over Canada, Mexico and Panama. We had high hopes of emulating the 'Reggae Boys' of Jamaica who made it to the finals in France in 1998.

We started off in blazing form in our preliminary group in the Caribbean Zone, and on 4 March 2000 I had the honour of scoring my first goal at that level and the very first goal of that World Cup – the first goal in over 800 matches that ended with Brazil being crowned world champions in the Far East. I will never forget that header at the back post from an in-swinging free-kick, nine minutes into that 5–0 demolition of Netherlands Antilles.

We went on to beat Mexico 1–0 at home – which was a tremendous result because they were one of the best teams in the world and the outstanding team in the CONCACAF, the Confederation of North, Central American and Caribbean Association Football, and had played in many World Cups. We topped the zone semi-final group and had a run that included a 6–0 win over Panama and a 4–0 victory against Canada – but Mexico got their revenge by humiliating us with a 7–0 hammering in Cuidad.

Our campaign completely fell apart because of things that happened off the pitch – the main one being miscommunication between Russell, Dwight and the management about them coming back on time. Dwight and Russell were late coming back, and the manager had a big dispute with them, all of which kicked in at the vital time when we needed one last big push to get to the finals.

After that, everything went downhill again. Our two top players retired from international football (although they came back later under a new coach). It was heartbreaking because we were playing so well and morale was destroyed by that one misunderstanding.

In the final round of the Caribbean zone, we played in

a mini-league with Costa Rica, Mexico, USA, Honduras and Jamaica – all teams we had played well against in previous tournaments. We were so demoralised that we won only one of our ten games, drew two and lost seven – a miserable performance – and our World Cup dream went on hold once again.

During the summer of 2002, I went home during the close season, which was also the time of the Japan/South Korea World Cup. I watched on TV as countries like South Korea and Costa Rica took part, and I knew we could have done just as well. I said then that the faster we got the administrative mess sorted out and got a good foundation for 2006, the better.

It was clear to me that the first priority had to be getting Dwight and Russell back in the T&T team. It was a great relief when CONCACAF supremo Jack Warner convinced them to end their international exile and Dwight was made captain.

In my first season for Rangers, in 2004, I took 12 flights across the Atlantic between August and December to play for T&T. Rangers manager Alex McLeish was very unhappy when I was forced to miss a game against Celtic for a T&T World Cup qualifier against St Vincent and the Grenadines. It was played on a Wednesday and the Old Firm game was on the Saturday. Shaka Hislop had been excused to play for Portsmouth against Manchester City in the Premiership, but they said there was no cover for me. Alex had been told it was a game T&T would win easily, and St Vincent needed to win 3–0 to pip us for a place in the next qualifying round.

I was always under pressure in the club-or-country stand-off, and several times I had to deny reports (which originated in Scotland) that I was prepared to turn my back on T&T football. I said, 'My dream and my goal is to play in a World Cup. I have been looking at this World Cup here and saying that I can play in it. My time is coming. I'm believing and I'm praying to God that it will happen.'

Mind you, there was at least one occasion when I seriously wondered whether all the travel back and forth across the Atlantic and around the Caribbean was worth it. I have now travelled hundreds of thousands of miles for football, but one particular flight stands out as the scariest of them all. Luckily, I was half-asleep through most of it . . .

I was coming back from a game in Costa Rica on a flight to Miami after a World Cup qualifier when a mate told me there was smoke in the cabin and the plane was on fire. I was thinking 'He's joking' so I just laughed. Half an hour later, I jumped up out of my sleep to find the plane was about to land. I looked out of the window and saw it wasn't Miami but a tiny airfield. The captain announced we had to make an emergency landing because of a problem with the plane. That's when I knew we were in trouble. I said a prayer and kept praying until we got down safely.

It was like being in the New Testament story of Jesus and his disciples in the boat. Jesus was sleeping and a storm made the disciples sore afraid until the Lord rebuked the wind and everything calmed down. To me, being on that plane was just like being one of those helpless disciples.

When we were on the ground, I thanked the Lord that everyone had been delivered safely. I looked on it as an attempt by the Devil to destroy us, but God had protected us. I have to say, I was glad that, while most of the drama was going on, I was asleep in the arms of the Lord!

Everything changed for the better for T&T with the appointment of Leo Beenhakker, the Dutchman with the immense reputation. During 40 years as a coach, he had won titles and honours for clubs like Ajax, Saragossa and Real Madrid (where he had won three successive league championships and the Spanish Cup), as well as coached clubs in Switzerland, Mexico and Turkey and the international teams of the Netherlands and Saudi Arabia.

Obviously, he was an experienced tactician, but what made him special was his man-management. Talking with my fellow players after our first few outings and training-ground sessions under Leo, we all agreed that, in a very short time, he had brought a new level of professionalism and organisation; he sparked a revival and restored our self-belief that we could compete at the highest level.

Rarely seen without a cigar between his teeth, he was fun to listen to. He obviously enjoyed what he called 'the wonderful, wild jungle of football', but there were years of wisdom behind everything he said about the game.

He showed he meant business from the moment he arrived. There was controversy in Trinidad (and some consternation among the players) when the first thing he did in May 2005 was call us together a month before our opening World Cup qualifier – and set up four friendlies in three weeks. Critics were talking about the danger of exhausting the team before we started the serious games! But, of course, Leo knew what he was doing.

Unbiased international experts commented that we

looked 'a picture of organisation' in the Caribbean-zone opener against Panama – something new for a team that had often lacked order. That was the Beenhakker effect.

The group stages were tough, especially against Mexico, the US and Guatemala; we took a few maulings and only took one point from the first three matches of the final group. We failed to make automatic qualification but forced ourselves into a play-off place on one fantastic night in Port of Spain.

There was despair all round when Stern John missed a first-half penalty against Mexico – but how he made up for it! The despair when we went one down turned to delirium when he equalised and then scored the winner and play-off clincher with a long-range shot. For the last 30 minutes, it was a case of putting the shutters up and defying the Mexicans.

The dramatic two-legged play-off against Bahrain was another tactical triumph for Leo Beenhakker. After drawing 1–1 at home, we went to Bahrain knowing we had one last chance. It was a hot, stifling night, playing in front of a hostile and fanatical crowd, and there was an early setback when Chris Birchall, who had been a hero in the first leg, limped off injured. But after four minutes of the second half, Dennis Lawrence headed in a Dwight Yorke corner to put us ahead. After that, defence was all-important.

The day we qualified against Bahrain, the smallest nation ever to reach that stage, was the greatest day of my football life. The dream I had been holding for 16 years to play for my country in the World Cup finals had been achieved. It was also a major victory for the organisation, confidence and team unity created by Leo Beenhakker in just six months. After that, we could not wait to get to Germany to play in the same group as England, Sweden and Paraguay.

Leo's relentless pursuit of perfection continued, and this time there was no criticism of his programme of 11 friendlies against a variety of clubs and countries between February and the World Cup finals in Germany in June.

In the week before the tournament proper, we lost a warm-up match against the Czech Republic, but the coach told us not to worry. He said he had deliberately chosen to have tough games versus Slovenia and the Czech Republic to get us used to the faster and more physical European game. We knew these matches would be difficult, but they gave us the experience, and we knew what to expect in the matches to come.

From Prague, we flew to Germany for the finals – and an astonishing reception. We were based in Rotenburg, and the mayor personally escorted us on the 40-minute journey from Bremen and gave us an official welcome reception on a stage in the city square. We were all asked to sign the city's golden book, and they took our nickname 'Soca Warriors' seriously, with gifts of ancient spears and arrows.

We were told that Rotenburg had been transformed into 'Little Trinidad' for the duration, and it certainly looked like it. The 3,000 people in the city square were mostly Germans, with a few Trinidadians who had arrived by charter, and they were all waving both German and T&T flags. Every other building had our national flag hanging from it. We were greeted by steel drums, and the team bus had the slogan 'Here Come the Soca Warriors'. Wherever we went, there were children and adults wearing our T-shirts with the logo 'Small country, big dream'. One touch that made us feel really at home was that when the team took the field in the tournament proper, our mascots were German schoolchildren, who went out with the players dressed in our T&T strips.

I was not surprised when word reached us that many Scots were supporting T&T. Of course, I knew the main reason was that we were drawn against England, when Scotland had not made it to the finals. But I also knew it was because of the number of Trinidadians playing for Scottish clubs – and there was always the presence of Jason Scotland, who allowed Scots to boast 'We're supporting Scotland!'

Then, just two days before our first game in the tournament, disaster struck for me. I went over during training and fell awkwardly and hurt my knee – the same knee, not the old injury but a new one. There were prophets of doom who, ever since I refused to have surgery on the cruciate ligament, had been predicting that my knee would break down. Up to that point, everything had been all right. My managers were happy with my fitness and I had no problems, even though I played on different surfaces, including AstroTurf. In Germany, the manager had picked the team, we were doing our shaping-up exercises and were about to travel the next morning. It was just one of those strains that can happen to any player in training.

I went to hospital with Doctor Terence Babwah Andrews and did some recovery work indoors trying to better the strained knee. Leo Beenhakker said he could wait right up until 24 hours before our first match, but in the end it was decided it was too much of a risk for the team, who were facing such an important test. He told a media conference, 'I've been waiting and hoping. Normally,

Marvin would be one of my starting eleven. He wants to play and is proud to represent his country. But what I've seen here isn't the Marvin I know. It's just little things with his knee, but he needs more time to recover.'

I was told it would take seven days, and that ruled me out of the games against Sweden and England. I was back for the Paraguay game but, unfortunately, never got a chance to get on. It was a disappointment, because to play in the World Cup finals is the ultimate for any player. I did not feel it as deeply as people thought I would, and the reason was that I had fulfilled my dream and helped to get my country to the finals. These things happen for a reason. I look at it that the Lord took me there before and He can take me there again.

England and Sweden were the heavyweights in Group B, and we were under no illusions about who the underdogs were. We were also determined that we would not disgrace our country or ourselves. Leo Beenhakker put it memorably: 'On paper, we know we are supposed to lose against Sweden. But football is not played on paper; it is played on a pitch. This game is not mathematics, and in football two plus two very rarely equals four – it's usually three or five.'

So we were not surprised, although everybody else was, when T&T gave an inspired performance, holding Sweden to a 0–0 draw and giving England a real scare. Again, Leo's tactics had made the most of our forward flair and our determined defence. T&T were disciplined, kept their shape, tackled hard and were not intimidated against a team that included players such as Freddie Ljungberg and Henrik Larsson. The 0–0 draw was deserved, and I know it caused a lot of heart-searching in the Sweden camp about why they could not break us down. They had not expected that Dwight Yorke, famous for being an attacker, would lie deep and defend so brilliantly. Switching from a forward to play as a deep-lying midfielder, Dwight did it so well that he was named as the best defender in the group games. The statistics showed that he topped the rankings in terms of successful tackles made. Shaka Hislop played out of his skin and pulled off crucial save after save. He wasn't even supposed to play, because Kelvin Jack of Dundee was the first choice that day, but he pulled his calf muscle in the warm-up. Typically, when he was told that he was unbeatable, Shaka said modestly, 'I didn't have any really good saves to make because the team defended very well.'

To get a point on the board in our first-ever game at that level was a magnificent achievement. It justified our being there after so many people had written us off, saying we probably wouldn't get a single point.

Then we held England until the last seven minutes, and only goals by Peter Crouch in the 83rd minute and Steven Gerrard in stoppage time saved them from what would have been a major embarrassment for English football. Crouch, who had missed several chances, met David Beckham's right-wing cross to power a header past Shaka. Brent Sancho, who is a Rasta with the full dreadlocks, claimed that he could not get to the cross because Crouch was pulling his hair! There was some debate about that, but Crouch is so tall he was able to jump over Sancho and score. Gerrard's goal was an absolute peach and very typical of him – a stunning, left-foot strike from the edge of the penalty box that no goalie could have stopped, not even our Shaka.

Gerrard had a habit of scoring fantastic goals against

Shaka. Two months earlier, he had a stunner in the FA Cup final, lashing in a last-minute equaliser that allowed Liverpool to beat West Ham on penalties. For some reason, Steven just seemed to have the hex on Shaka.

With a little bit more luck, we could have got another point or two, but the bigger teams seem to get all the luck. The doggedness of our team, though, was proven by the fact that our group ended up having the lowest number of goals scored in it, although it had been expected that England and Sweden would run riot. For T&T to hold its own in such a group and give these major football countries such a fright proved that we were there by right, on skill, talent and our commitment, and we were not just there making up the numbers. It said a lot for our football.

I was so proud of all my countrymen. That is why I am sure we will be back again at future World Cup finals and I know we will acquit ourselves well, no matter which countries we are drawn against. The FIFA official assessment says it all:

> It may have been their first-ever appearance at this level, but Trinidad and Tobago surprised more than a few observers. Their lively team play was a joy to behold.
>
> Trinidad and Tobago can also be satisfied with their performance at their first-ever FIFA World Cup. They gave an excellent account of themselves, and both the players and the fans can feel justly proud of their team, which showed that they were capable of holding their own with the big guns.
>
> Indeed, with a bit more luck throughout the tournament, who knows how far they could have gone?

We are now legends for ever in Trinidad. When you land at the Piarco International Airport, it is our pictures that greet you.

Even after a century of caps, I have not lost my desire. I will chase my World Cup dream for T&T until I can't walk anymore, can't play anymore.

Chapter Six

PLAYING THE BEAUTIFUL GAME

Youngsters all over the world start out kicking a football in the street or on any patch of open ground. They all have their football heroes and dream of being like them. So what allows a few – and it is just a few, compared with the millions who play and love the game – to make it to the big leagues and international honours?

In my case, I readily admit that the Lord gave me the physical attributes to make my mark on the field. But it is about a lot more than your size, build or even natural talent.

My own experience teaches me that young footballers will not progress unless they get the right coaching from an early age, developing the talents they have, instilling tactical and team sense, teaching them the right attitudes and giving them confidence in themselves.

And no player is going to get to the top without that inbuilt competitive mindset, the will to win and never-say-die approach that always insists there is something to play for, right up to the last kick.

Call it big-headed if you like, but I also believe that the game is not worth playing unless you enjoy putting your skills on display and giving the crowd something to cheer. Although they may not admit it, all the best players are like that.

And I would always be the first to admit that luck plays a big part . . .

When it comes to my own football career, nothing has happened because of planning or seeking out opportunities to promote myself. Good fortune and God's guidance have given me a life beyond my wildest dreams. In fact, if someone else had not seen something special in me and given me a push in the right direction (a push I didn't really want at the time), I would probably still be working in the brewery in Trinidad, having a good time with my mates and playing semi-pro football but not really achieving very much.

For me, football was just a kick-about game until I went to secondary school; in many countries nowadays, scouts for major clubs are spotting potential future stars at that age and signing them up on S-forms (which fairly commit promising youngsters to particular teams). But, like most boys, I just played for fun; I had never taken the game seriously and certainly never thought I could make a living from it. I was always big for my age, and it was no surprise that the sports teacher at my secondary school, Mount Hope, should mark me out for the football team. I was happy to be recognised, but it was always my dream to be a striker, playing up front and scoring goals. Because of my size, though, standing head and shoulders above most youngsters my age, I suppose it was inevitable that the school coach should convert me into a defender. Also, I am the first to admit that I have never been the fastest player on the field! But I still get a big personal boost out of scoring goals whenever I can; I always go up for corners and set pieces, and, for a central defender, I think I have notched up a pretty respectable scoring tally.

Moving up to the San Juan senior comprehensive, I didn't push to get into the school team. Although my schoolmates were egging me on, I did not have any confidence and did not believe I had any special talent. It took a lot for me to try for the team in my final year – and, as I have said, I was really lucky that the coach was Miguel Hackett. Under Miguel, I not only learned how to be a defender, but, more importantly, I learned a lot about being more confident, more competitive and more committed. To this day, when I am on the field, these lessons are still with me.

If I had a special talent, it was my ability to be first to a high ball and head it back deep into the opponents' half. I have no idea where this came from, but from an early age, if the other goalie booted a clearance anywhere near me, I was able to meet a ball dropping out of the sky and head it back 40 yards or more.

People were amazed, and it became something of a trademark, although some were worried for me that I might injure myself. I was still a developing boy, and I am just glad it wasn't in the days of the old, heavy leather balls, otherwise who knows what damage I might have done to myself?

Other boys, who had started in football earlier than me, had already represented Trinidad in the Under-14 and Under-16 teams. I still had no great thoughts about winning a cap, and I only began to wake up to the possibilities of becoming something in the game when I was screened for the national Under-18 team and I began training seriously.

Being chosen to wear the T&T colours at the age of 17

was a milestone in my life and my football career. I knew that, from then on, football would be a major part of my life and I really wanted to achieve something in the game – although I still had no serious ambitions about becoming a full-time professional, far less playing for a senior club in another country.

When my football achievements began to be noticed and I was asked to join Carib FC, a good team with high standards, and given a job in the sponsoring company's brewery, I really thought I had it made, and I never considered the prospect of making more money and getting more fame.

What more could a young guy want? Being paid as a part-time football player with prospects of getting into the full international side, plus a full-time job in a brewery and all the lager you could drink – life was good. After all, I had achieved the height of many a young Trinidadian's ambition!

You can imagine what a wrench it was when the brewery manager called me in and told me he had bought me a plane ticket to go and become a full-time professional in Scotland. I will always be grateful to Mr Nafziger, but it was a big decision for me, and I was very reluctant to leave my pleasant lifestyle for the challenge of playing football in a strange country where I knew no one.

That move literally took me up into a different league. When I left Trinidad, I had my natural attributes and a good, sound grounding in the game. Moving to Scotland – and also working under the succession of British and European coaches in the T&T international side – turned me into a better, more experienced and effective player altogether.

Management, coaching and tactics do make the difference between honest, hard-working effort on the football field and real success. It is one thing to have flashes of brilliance, but what is really needed is a consistently high standard of play, and that is what coaching, concentration and personal dedication give you. Also, it is only when you play among top players that you realise how much you are learning from them, both from your teammates and your opponents. Believe me, the best players are willing to learn more about the game right up to the end of their careers.

When I go onto the pitch, I'm a winner. I play hard and strong. My teammates will tell you I am always out to win, to do the best for the team and give my all to everything I do on the field. Sometimes in Scotland, managers have even told me before going out on the training ground not to go through any of my teammates! Not that I would have, of course, but it showed that they knew all about my commitment whenever I'm on the field.

I never go out with the aim of damaging anyone or destroying anyone's career, but I have that strong desire to win. If I mistime a tackle or a challenge or kick someone, that is never the intention. My objective is always to win the ball or play my part as a defender to stop opponents from scoring.

I don't have the mentality to hurt another player. I look at it as 'You are a professional, trying to make a living and help your family. I am a professional, trying to do the same, so why should we go at each other with the intention of damaging each other?' But when you try to win headers in the air, with big men on either side challenging whole-heartedly for 50–50 balls, people are bound to get hurt.

A dedicated friend and fan back in Trinidad has kept scrapbooks of my career, and when I look at the newspaper photographs over the years, the most noticeable thing is that I always seem to be in mid-air or jumping shoulder-to-shoulder for a high ball or in the middle of a pile of players – although the ones I enjoy most are when we are celebrating. What these pictures show is that the Scottish game is hard and physical, and, to be a winner, you have to give 100 per cent.

But I always get a sick feeling in my stomach when I clash with an opponent and he is left hurt. Even when it has been entirely unintentional, I feel I have to pray for forgiveness for my part in causing injury to another player.

In March 2001, when I was playing for Livingston, I felt particularly bad after an accidental collision of heads left Ayr United's Marvyn Wilson with a fractured jaw which required an operation to insert a metal plate. It was a ferociously fought 1–1 draw with a lot of aerial battles against the Ayr forwards, particularly Marvyn. I am not the kind of person to do such a thing intentionally. Some people seemed to think I should not have gone in so forcefully and that I had deliberately head-butted Marvyn and broken his jaw – but that is not in my nature, and it is not how I think football should be played. As soon as it happened, my heart went out to him. I later sent him my regrets, and I prayed for him to recover as quickly as possible. Immediately after, Marvyn said himself, 'I'm not going to start badmouthing the big man. I know he's totally committed to his team. It was just one of those things. I have no grudges, and I don't think he was being malicious.'

I thought that was very fair of him, especially when he was suffering and had just been told he would be out of the game for at least a month.

Just as there are national characteristics, there are national football styles, and everyone recognises that those of us who are from the Caribbean play with joy in our hearts. There is a real contradiction in professional football. There is so much at stake commercially that it has become a really serious business – yet the best football is played when players are enjoying themselves on the field. You have a professional job to do, but you need not be grim about it. You have to enjoy your job to perform at your highest level. You need concentration, but you should not be thinking you have to tackle a player so hard you will damage him or be in despair when you miss a chance at goal.

I am glad to say this was shown from the very beginning by Arthur Wharton, who was thought to be the world's first black professional footballer in the 1880s. Born in Ghana, he moved to England to train as a Methodist preacher and proved himself an enormously gifted athlete. He was a first-class goalkeeper, a professional cricketer, a record-breaking cyclist, a boxer and held the world 100-yard sprint record when he won the AAA championship in exactly ten seconds. He was also the first footballer-showman, who would amuse the crowd with tricks like hanging from the crossbar and catching the ball with his feet or lying on the goal line for a rest before sprinting out to block the striker bearing down on him. A touching postscript to his amazing career was that he died penniless after working down the mines in Yorkshire, and it was only recently that his grave got a headstone, through the Professional Footballers'

Association (PFA) and Football Unites, Racism Divides.

If only football could make room for more players with Arthur Wharton's joyous approach. I have seen players whose attitude to every game was life and death, because, in a sense, week after week, you live or die by results. Everybody wants to win, but if there is no enjoyment in playing the game, you will struggle to be successful.

Caribbean and South American players have the same positive approach. Ronaldinho, the best player in the world, plays with that sense of enjoyment, and you can see he just loves playing the game. Even at his level, he may hit a shot that goes 50 yards over the bar and he will smile, thank God and go on. There are other players who, when they do that, are kicking themselves and cursing. We should accept that even top football players are all human beings and will all make mistakes. An old manager told me, 'You can never be perfect. You hear people say "practice makes perfect". Not so – practice makes permanent.' I recognised the truth of that: you can do something every day and it will become consistent. You can get really good at it, but every so often you will mishit the ball or mistime the tackle and it goes wrong.

I have heard it said about me: 'When Marvin is good, he is very, very good – but when he is bad, he's awful!' The fans pay their money and they expect to see you play at a certain level all the time, but it doesn't always work like that. I take comfort from the fact that the best players in the world make mistakes and are still rated the best. They are not perfect – but they are the ones who keep trying. If you are not enjoying it, you will not try.

Even when I spend a match sitting on the substitutes' bench and the only exercise I get is the occasional warm-up run down the touchline, the fans will still see me smiling. They are the paying customers, and they do not deserve to see a sour-faced player who does not interact with them.

Many managers do not understand that. Davie Hay at Livingston and Alex McLeish at Rangers taught me not to get tetchy when the manager drops you. It isn't because he thinks you are no good or he has turned against you; it is because the tactics demand it, or he thinks you need a rest to protect you from damage, or maybe he just wants to see how you will react.

I was signed for a particular role – a very physical role, especially in Old Firm games – and I had no problem with that. People always have something to say, and many believed I was not good enough for Rangers. Even my good friend Barry Ferguson thought I was not a good signing at the time. Many thought I would not play too often, except when the club needed someone to go up against strong, hard Celtic players like Hartson and Balde. Then I was part of the championship-winning side and was chosen as the Players' Player of the Year. And not long after I left Ibrox, the same people were saying they wanted me back at Rangers.

I enjoy the glory of that, but I take no personal credit for it because my destiny is not in my hands or the hands of any human being. I am the first to admit that I do not have the ability or the skills of some players – but I have God, and the little that I have, God can make great.

Football is, of course, a team game, but, for me, the most important member of the team is the coach or manager. God has brought me coaches who spurred me on and brought out the best in me at every level. I have already mentioned my coach Keith LokLoy in Trinidad. He was so committed he would shout, swear, even hit you. But, because of him, I became aggressive and my belief in myself became strong. If I had not had his influence, I would not have been strong enough to hold my own when I came to Scotland and then go on to a higher standard.

In Scotland, I have had forceful, hard-driving coaches who would shout and rage when their players had had a bad game or made a mistake. That does not mean they disliked us or were being abusive; they do it to help us become better players. My fellow players may not like this comparison, but it can be like training a child; there will be times when you praise and times when you have to talk in a stern manner. If a manager does not chide you when you get it wrong in training or turn up late, he is not doing his job and is increasing the chances of failure.

The bigger the club, the more professionalism I have found. Good managers also know the pressures that come with maintaining the standards of a top club. Anywhere you go, even when you go to the supermarket, you are carrying the whole club with you. People do not see just your personal identity, because you are known as that Rangers or Celtic or Manchester United player. Some players find that hard – especially when they are going about their everyday life or trying to relax in a social atmosphere and are challenged in a nasty or menacing way by fans of a rival club. It is something you have to learn to live with and handle in a relaxed way.

Chapter Seven

KICK OUT THE RACISTS

Racism of any kind is evil. It has no place anywhere and certainly not in sport. That is why I joined up with the Show Racism the Red Card campaign, and my message was, 'Racism tries to destroy everything good in the world. You can't judge someone by the colour of their skin, their origin, or because they come from a different nation or religion, especially in football. Scottish football has to stamp racism out.'

It was very special for me to join the same campaign as players such as Henrik Larsson, who said, 'You have to look beyond race because, as a human being, you have to experience the person inside the skin.' The colour of your skin has never been an issue in Trinidad, where white people have been born and brought up as part of the population. And I can honestly say that, all the time I have been in Scotland, my colour has never been an issue and I have never directly experienced racial abuse.

I'm not a great pub or club person, but when I have gone in with my mates and had a Coke, I have never had anybody raise the issue of race. If they had something to say, it would be about football, such as 'You're no good' or 'You were rubbish'. They are entitled to their opinion, and if you are a player, you have to expect that and deal with it.

There may have been times when opposing fans have made racial remarks, but nothing has ever reached my ears. In fact, I was surprised when I was at Livingston to read in the paper that some guy had been locked up for racial abuse against me and Eugene Dadi, because I hadn't heard even one thing he'd said.

Perhaps those who shout such things should realise that either the player who is the target of their abuse is concentrating so much on the game that he is oblivious to their insults or there is so much noise coming from the terraces that you cannot hear the oddballs. But it can cause trouble on the terracing or in the stand if other fans are offended.

The St Johnstone supporter (I won't dignify him by naming him) who called me a 'black bastard' in October 2003 was prosecuted and fined £450. He tried to justify it by telling the court, 'I am a passionate supporter of my own team. Saying that players are rubbish is part and parcel of football.' I would not have minded if he had said I was rubbish – any fan who has paid for his ticket has the right to his opinion – but he does not have the right to be racially offensive. I appreciate that people who are passionate about the game or their particular team say things in the heat of the moment that they don't really mean, but they are offensive nonetheless.

No matter who you are or where you come from, you should always treat others the way you would like to be treated. The colour of your skin should not matter; it's the person inside that counts.

When he played for Dundee, Brent Sancho – my colleague in the T&T World Cup team – found himself in the middle of a well-publicised incident that took place *off* the field. Brent told a court that a man had called him a 'black bastard' and a 'f****** nigger' while waiting at a taxi rank. He was on trial with Steven McNally for allegedly assaulting the man, who was a former bouncer. Both players were found not guilty. Brent said, 'I personally hadn't suffered anything like that before, thank God, but I know racism does exist; it definitely does exist.'

He said it was becoming more obvious during football games: 'It is more introverted than extroverted these days. But a lot of the problem is due to fans who go off the hinges in supporting their teams.'

People will try to use all kinds of things to upset you, and I have heard some very bad stories about specific places in England, but I have never personally experienced discrimination, physical or verbal, and never heard a racial comment against me. I know there were incidents with big Bobo Balde of Celtic, when idiots in the crowd were chanting 'monkey'. That isn't good for any part of the world, no matter your colour, because it can happen to a white person in a black nation. We know it's out there because it is happening to people of different skin colours every day.

When I left Trinidad for Scotland, I never had the slightest concern that I might be attacked as a black person in a white nation. From watching English Premiership and Continental games on TV back home, it was clear that black players were now accepted and appreciated. I watched black British stars such as Viv Anderson, the first 'official' black footballer to play for England and now a respected coach; Garth Crooks, who gained full England international honours, has been a media figure, ex-chairman of the PFA and received the OBE for his work for sport and medical charities; and the tragic Laurie Cunningham, the 'Black Pearl', the first black player to win an England Under-21 cap and graduate to the senior side, and who was a Real Madrid regular before being killed in a car accident at the age of only 33. They were all role models for me, but also to young players of any colour. But there is always an undercurrent . . .

I had known about racism in America from the days of Martin Luther King, things like the Ku Klux Klan and the struggle against discrimination when a black person could not sit down where he wanted on a bus. Racism is another example of how the Devil works. The Devil knows unity is strength, that God has created people of all colours and that this is what makes the world such a great and glorious place. Beneath the skin, we are all the same – we all have the same nose, eyes, limbs, brain, senses and vital organs.

The Devil does not want black and white to be together. I like to point out that, yes, black and white are opposite colours, but when they are worn together – such as a black suit and a white shirt – that is the best colour coordination you can have!

The Bible teaches that God looks at the heart and not at the outward appearance of a human being. It is the Devil who makes a person of one race look at another and say, 'I do not like him because of the colour of his skin.'

The furore about the *Celebrity Big Brother* programme showed how the Devil can get into a person and cause havoc. The programme caught the attention of the international media because of what was seen as racist behaviour and bullying of the Bollywood star Shilpa

Shetty. It was astonishing that some ill-advised words, spoken in ignorance in the heat of the moment, became so notorious. The girls who spoke those words forgot they were not just talking within the walls of the Big Brother house, they were being viewed by millions of people across the world. Jade Goody, in particular, became a hate-figure. She may not be as bad as she seemed, but the Devil got into her mind and made her say those offensive things. God said you will be judged by your words, and she was judged to be a racial bigot.

It was interesting that what she said was racist *and* foul-mouthed – but few people seem to have been offended by her cursing and blasphemy. The language she used showed that, although she is a so-called 'celebrity', she is really a rude young woman. Such people always reach for the most obvious insult, which happened to be Shilpa Shetty's race.

Unfortunately, in sport – and, it seems, especially in football – it is just too easy for someone in the crowd to single out a player because of colour. They may really be wanting to show their opposition to his team or trying to insult the colours he is wearing, but in their ignorance they grasp at the easiest thing to abuse, and the most identifiable thing is the colour of his skin. People in football crowds get carried away and say things that they would regret if they thought about it.

A bad experience of one person does not mean you can condemn everybody who is of the same colour or race. A lot of it comes down to knowledge and experience. The more we travel, the more we experience different cultures and nationalities. Football teams bring together players of different races, who cooperate and play for each other. That is unity at work, like all the different parts of the one body working together. We are created in different colours, with differently shaped eyes, heads, noses, etc., but we are all created in God's image. And, as the great Eusebio said, 'Black or white, we all have football under our skin.'

As I have said, I have not directly experienced racism, but I know it has been a problem in Scotland, although nowhere near as bad as in other countries. I believe I owe a debt of gratitude to those who paved the way and made it easier for my generation to be accepted for what we are – professional footballers who happen to have a different skin colour.

The history of coloured players in Scotland is interesting. Mark Walters is thought of as the first black player in Scottish football; certainly, he was the first of the modern era when he signed for Rangers in 1987 and became the first coloured player in the SPL.

Almost forgotten, except by historians, are the real pioneers from a much earlier age. Recent research has thrown up the startling discovery that the first black professional footballer in Britain was almost certainly Andrew Watson. He was also the first black soccer international, because he was capped three times for Scotland between 1881 and 1882. Born in British Guiana, Andrew Watson went to Glasgow University to study for a bachelor of arts degree and played for Queen's Park, the Glasgow club which was then the most famous amateur team. He married and settled with his wife and family in Govan, not far from where Rangers play now. He was much sought after as 'one of the best players in Britain', and when he played for London Swifts, he became the first black player to compete in the FA Cup. As secretary of Queen's Park, this remarkable man also became the first black football administrator – something to think about as we wait for more coloured players to become managers and coaches.

When I joined Glasgow Rangers, I knew about Mark Walters but I did not know I was the latest in a line of coloured players for the club that stretched back nearly a century! The first was meant to have been a remarkable character called Walter Tull, who was on the verge of signing for Rangers when he was killed in the First World War. For someone like me, his is an inspiring story. The grandson of a slave in Barbados, he played wing-half for Tottenham Hotspur and Northampton Town between 1910 and 1914, when Rangers offered what was then a huge transfer fee for him. With the outbreak of war, the move was put on hold, and Walter enlisted. Despite military regulations forbidding 'any negro or person of colour' being an officer, he became the first-ever black officer in the British army. He led his men at the Battle of Piave in Italy and died in an attack on the German trenches on the Western Front in France in 1918. It says a lot for his qualities as a man and a leader that several of his men made valiant efforts under heavy fire from German machine guns to bring him back to the British trenches.

Nearly 20 years later, Rangers did acquire their first coloured player when they signed Mohamed Latif, a Muslim from Egypt who was studying at Jordanhill College in Glasgow. He was an attacking winger and must have been a first-class player because he played for Egypt in the 1936 Olympics and was given a three-year contract by Rangers. He was also popular with the Ibrox fans, who called him 'Hammie' or 'Eejupt', but I wonder what they thought when he began to teach in Glasgow – at a Roman Catholic school . . .

About the same time, Celtic had an Asian player on the fringes of their first team: Abdul-Salim Bachi Khan, a steward with a Scottish shipping line who had played at home in Calcutta and was said to be an Indian international. On his regular visits to Glasgow, he told his brother, who had settled in the city, that he missed playing football. The brother asked the famous Celtic manager Willie Maley to give him a trial, and he turned out in the Alliance League for Celtic Reserves against Galston and Hamilton Academicals, against whom he scored a penalty. It has been reported that Salim chose not to wear the heavy football boots that were worn in Scotland in those days and played in those matches with tightly bandaged feet, as was his local custom in India. I am not sure if I really believe that, but it is a good story – and has become a football legend. One reason for doubting it is that it was said he thrilled the crowds with the way he could trap the ball and launch it towards goal, and he was noted for his hard shot. As a defender, I do not imagine that his opponents would pull back in the tackle just because he was wearing bandages! If the story is true, he was taking a big risk.

Earlier, there was an Egyptian, Tewfik 'Toothpick' Abdullah, who played in bare feet for Sporting Club Cairo and the Egyptian army, but when he signed for Derby County in 1920 he quickly made the switch to boots.

Another player who gets overlooked is Jamaican-born Giles Heron, who was spotted by Celtic in 1951 when they were on an American tour and he was playing for Detroit Corinthians. A sporting all-rounder who also boxed, played cricket and ice hockey, he played centre-forward for the Jamaican national football team and was so speedy he was nicknamed the 'Black Flash'. He scored in his first game for Celtic, a 2–1 win against Morton, but was released after only one season and went to Third Lanark. Somehow, he rarely gets a mention in football histories and is best remembered as the father of jazz musician and poet Gil Scott-Heron, who is credited as a founding father of rap.

These players were regarded as rarities, and it was not until the late 1970s that black players became significant in British professional football. It really began with the immigrants arriving from the British colonies in the 1950s and '60s, and when the next generation came along, they started to make their presence felt right across the sporting spectrum. Especially interesting to me is the fact that these players may have been regarded with curiosity but they were accepted without any suggestion of colour prejudice.

Mark Walters was not so lucky. Although black players were generally accepted when Rangers signed him from Aston Villa in 1987, racism had become an inflamed issue in Britain. It was certainly an issue for a small minority of the Ibrox supporters, and some season-ticket holders were banned following racist abuse aimed at Mark. They certainly did not represent the majority, because he was a favourite of the Rangers support, was made an honorary member of the Rangers Supporters Trust and has continued to receive a big welcome playing in Masters football tournaments for Rangers. It was brave of Mark to make the move to become the first-ever black player in the Scottish Premier Division – and brave of Rangers' chairman David Murray and manager Graeme Souness, who deserve full credit for breaking down the barriers of race and of sectarianism, as they did with the signing of Mo Johnston, the former Celtic player.

It is shocking to be reminded that Mark was subjected to racist abuse from his debut appearance. In his first Old Firm game, some Celtic supporters dressed up in monkey suits and threw bananas at him, and the second half of the game was held up so that the Parkhead ground staff could clear the fruit from the pitch. They may have thought that was a clever joke (they must have gone to some trouble to get the costumes); in fact, they were showing their ignorance and adding another type of bigotry to the sort that already polluted these games. Gerry Britton, who was a 16-year-old Celtic apprentice at the time and went on to become a manager, said later, 'I was appalled at the hideous racist goading of Rangers' black winger Mark Walters during his Old Firm debut at Celtic Park.

'I was even more sickened on the morning after the match when I was told to help clear the Parkhead trackside of the dozens of bananas that had been thrown onto the field by so-called Celtic supporters intent on upsetting the on-field focus of the Ibrox wing wizard.'

Following on from Mark, Scottish football has seen a procession of coloured players from England and abroad. In fact, it is hard to think of an SPL club that does not have a black player on its books, and I had no qualms about coming to Scotland because I knew players, such as my friend and fellow Trinidadian Russell Latapy, had been accepted and were doing well.

As is well known, Scotland has large Asian and Chinese communities but until recently very few from African or Caribbean backgrounds. That explains why it was not until 2003 that a Scottish-born black player was chosen to play for his country: Kevin Harper, who was born and brought up in Glasgow. Even Kevin encountered prejudice, in the land of his birth. When he was playing for Hibs in an Edinburgh derby against Hearts, he claimed he suffered racist abuse, but when the matter was reported to the Scottish Football Association (SFA), no action was taken. Kevin, who is now a businessman in Glasgow, said he felt let down by the governing body: 'There was video evidence and nothing got done about it. If you want to sweep things like that under the carpet, then they will come back and bite you.'

Kevin went on to have a successful career in the English Premiership, playing for Derby County and the Portsmouth side that included Yakubu, Shaka Hislop and Nigel Quashie. A fast, forceful and clever winger, Kevin seemed just the player Scotland needed, and Bertie Vogts picked him for the international side but kept him on the bench.

So the honour of becoming the first modern-era black player to get a full Scottish cap went to Nigel Quashie – who was born in England! Nigel had played for the English Under-21s, but, because his grandfather was born in Glasgow, he was able to opt for Scotland and became a regular first-choice midfielder for the national side. Nigel made his debut against Estonia, but it is his second appearance that I have cause to remember. It was in the friendly against T&T at Easter Road, Edinburgh, on 30 May 2004, and he scored one of Scotland's four goals against us.

So far, it is noticeable that there are no Asian players coming to the front rank in Scottish football – either as imports, or, more importantly, locally born. My old club, Livingston, pioneered Show Racism the Red Card to make facilities and coaching available to cross-cultural teams. One club in particular, Glasgow Ansar, which was formed in 2001 to provide a sporting platform for the mainly Asian ethnic minority youths on Glasgow's south side, were provided with coaching and training facilities at Almondvale stadium. The scheme is being extended to other clubs with the aim of getting more black and ethnic minority players to make the breakthrough into the professional game.

Rangers regularly scout the Asian leagues and run community programmes to attract youngsters of all backgrounds. They had one lad, Jazz Juttla, born in Glasgow of Indian descent, on their books, who dropped down to a junior side – but I am confident there will be more.

Another promising sign is that the children of asylum seekers have already started to appear in club academies, and Celtic have two at the Under-13 and Under-14 level in theirs who are already showing great promise. Cherif Lancine, a 15-year-old asylum seeker from the Ivory Coast who has no family in Scotland, was given a professional contract with Rangers after he was spotted playing with friends on a cinder pitch and given a try-out at Ibrox. As Bobo Balde of Celtic has said, 'Refugees are our fellow human beings and deserve to be treated as such. People should take the opportunity to find out the reasons that force people to leave their homes and reach out to asylum seekers and refugees who live with us.'

Encouraging youngsters from minorities is clearly a responsible and worthy thing to do, but clubs are also businesses, and it also makes commercial sense if they can tap into a grass-roots source of new players. The bottom line was spelt out by the anti-racism campaigner who said, 'It doesn't matter where someone is from or the colour of their skin, if they can score goals, then clubs will be interested.'

The next step will be to get more blacks and ethnic minorities into football management and coaching, just like my pal Russell Latapy, who is first-team coach at Falkirk. I know he intended to retire after the World Cup finals with T&T, which he thought would have been the perfect way to end his career at the age of 38. He decided not to hang up his boots when he was given the chance to play on and, at the same time, coach an SPL side. As well as teaching the players some of the tricks that have kept him at the top and made him a legend back home, he is still able to turn out and show them how it is done against tough opposition in the SPL!

The clear anti-racist policy in Scottish football is backed by the power of the law. But that alone will never end racism. The most the law can do is penalise people and make them stop and think, but these people just do not think, because they have hate in their hearts. Hateful attitudes have to be changed within the person and within their group.

Players like me have a duty, through campaigns like Show Racism the Red Card, to keep drawing attention to the danger of prejudice and bigotry raising their ugly heads in our sport. The game's authorities also have a duty to be more definite in taking action when complaints are made to them. There have been a couple of recent cases where clubs have complained about racist taunts by opposing players but the SFA have either found them 'not proven' or taken no action.

It was only after pressure from clubs and campaigners that the SFA announced that new measures would be introduced to deal with claims of on-field racist and sectarian abuse. There must never be any suspicion of complacency, or, even worse, that racism is being swept under the carpet.

When I go back to Trinidad, I tell everybody that Scottish people are friendly and welcoming to all races. Bigotry in Scottish football is conducted by a very tiny minority, and they are not true football fans. Scotland is a loving country and still a Christian nation. And, don't forget, Andrews is a famous Scottish name – so maybe I have ancestors from Scotland!

I am afraid that racism will always be there, as long as the Devil is on the earth. Racism may seem to disappear, and we may manage to educate our young people against it, but it will always rear its head, and we have to be ready to deal with it whenever and wherever it does.

Chapter Eight

GOD'S XI

Pelé once said, 'Football is like a religion to me. I worship the ball, and I treat it like a god.' I am sure he was not equating a game with true religion but just illustrating the dedication that is needed to achieve the kind of sublime skill he had. However, there are people to whom football *is* a religion. And some even make football an excuse for religious bigotry – and bring shame on the sport they claim to love.

There is a healthier way in which football and religion can come together. Whether we like it or not, footballers *do* set an example, for good or bad, and the media are now commenting on the number of high-profile footballers who speak openly about their faith.

One result was a national-newspaper feature under the headline 'God's XI'. I saw my picture on the page, along with a number of international players – but what was most amazing was that the goalie was the late Pope John Paul II, who had played football as a young man!

I was not the first openly Christian player in the Rangers dressing-room – Bert Kontermann, who is a firm believer, was there before me. Bert admitted there was a time when he got angry with the media and hated the way they were treating him. He explained how faith had helped him deal with that: 'I asked God to help me to forgive them, and He did that. I have no bad feelings towards the media any more.'

Juan Sara of Dundee is also a born-again Christian who has spoken openly about his belief – even though his faith was tested when he missed two penalties in a game against Rangers in 2001! Juan just said, 'That is life; it's only a game. I still believe in God, and maybe next time I will score for Him.'

A man I really respect in Scottish football is Tommy Burns, who has dedicated his career as player, manager and coach to Celtic and Scotland. He is also another who is not ashamed to show his belief in front of the crowd, and there is a famous photograph of Tommy on his knees on the pitch, hands clasped and eyes closed in prayer, giving thanks. To him, it is perfectly natural after a highly charged game that has ended in a title to give thanks to the person who gave him his talent and the opportunity to achieve. Others forget God and say it's because of the way they work and train, or it's because of their agent or their manager or their teammates.

God has given me the ability to play football in my particular way. I think nothing of outjumping opponents and heading the ball 30–40 yards because God has given me the physique and the capacity to do it. I have also worked on it, because, like anything else, it needs to be nurtured before it brings forth fruit. The parable of the talents tells us that you are given what is needed, but you have to put it to good use. I train hard and I work hard, but I remember to give thanks for the ability I have been given.

I am not saying that those players who are religious should always parade their beliefs in public. They should do it if they feel called to do it and feel comfortable with that. Sometimes, it can be asking for trouble; but it is good that a growing number of leading footballers have come forward and spoken about their faith.

The former English Premiership player Gavin Peacock – a committed Christian who is now a TV commentator – has drawn attention to the growing influence of religion among footballers. I was one of the players he featured in a special report for the BBC's *Football Focus* programme. He told me that when he was playing for Newcastle and Chelsea in the mid-'90s, there were ten Christian players throughout the Football League, and now there were six times that number.

Because of the worldwide search for talent to play in the English Premiership and the SPL, there are also a number of devout Muslim players. In practising their religion, they have to make sacrifices – including fasting during Ramadan, even when they are training and playing in matches. What impressed Gavin was that, in the increasingly secular society we live in, more footballers are saying there is something bigger in their lives than the sport they play.

Like me, Gavin has known highs and lows in his career. One season he was playing in European football and the next, after Ruud Gullit took over as manager, he found there was no place for him in the Chelsea team. The testimony on Gavin's website is valuable reading for anybody, but most especially for any young player. What he has written there could be used as a gospel for those hoping to make football their career. He says that, in football, you need something to help you keep a level head through the ups and downs, injuries, defeats and disappointments. These can be depressing if football is the true centre of your life. He believes that God gives you the sense of self-worth to carry you through those times.

Gavin and the others who featured on his programme know that by declaring themselves as Christians who happen to be footballers, they are setting themselves up to be judged by the public. We have to be seen giving our all on the pitch – and that includes not shrinking from tackles, as long as we are not deliberately trying to hurt an opponent, and when we are off the pitch, we have to remember that people are looking at us to see what kind of example we are setting.

It is not uncommon nowadays to see players saying a short prayer before the kick-off. We are not praying to win; we are dedicating the game to God and giving Him the glory. He has given us the talent and the ability to develop it and make something of it. We do not look on football success – good results and championship honours – as our success or even all our own effort. We are honouring God because He honours us.

In that same programme, the superbly talented Tottenham Hotspur and England player Jermain Defoe was asked why he needs God when he is already a rich young man at the age of 25. His reply was typically modest and made very good sense to me: 'I have been blessed, and I always show my appreciation because, without God, there is nothing, basically.'

Jermain has also noticed that there are many more Christians in football than there used to be: 'Obviously, it isn't the main subject in the dressing-room, but before a game you sit there and see teammates praying and you say, "That's really good. I didn't realise they were that type of person."'

From what Jermain said, it was clear that his faith helped him handle with dignity being left out of the England World Cup squad, when most people expected him to be an automatic choice. And when Gavin asked him straight out what was more important in his life, Jesus Christ or football, Jermain did not hesitate: 'Jesus Christ, most definitely.'

Linvoy Primus, the outgoing Portsmouth player, laughed when he remembered the reaction when he told his teammates he had become a Christian: 'I got some stick! It was "Are you weak? Are you not strong enough?"'

Linvoy and I share the experience of a serious injury being healed through prayer – although, in his case, it was even more dramatic than my recovery. He said, 'I had a quite serious knee injury, and the guy that brought me into the church prayed. I felt something in my knee. It felt like electricity going through my knee and then there was no pain.

'The doctor said, "I guarantee you will be back in for this operation within a year." Nearly four years later, I still have not had that operation, and I am still playing.'

If anyone needs it, that is proof that the famous Marvin Andrews knee injury was not a freak or a one-off recovery. Prayer really *can* heal.

I found it really admirable that football players who are so high-profile should speak out so plainly for what they believe in, especially in these days when talking about religion and your individual faith is a kind of degraded thing.

We all know there are players who have brought football into disrepute by the way they have behaved in their own lives. There are some who are so misguided or so full of their own success that they just do not see how religion or belief in God in any form can help them. They have risen so high they say, 'Why do I need God? I'm a millionaire with all the material things and everything I could possibly need in life.'

Everybody knows what a footballing genius George Best was, and when you see recordings of him playing, it is obvious he had a powerful self-belief in his talent. If you ask any youngster if they know who Bestie was, they will tell you immediately that he was a fantastic player, but if you ask how he died, they will also be able to tell you: through drink. Sadly, he is known for both things. Perhaps, if George Best had managed to have more faith in God and less in his seeming belief that his football ability would see him through all his problems, he would be alive today and would not be remembered as such a tragic figure.

It is the same with sportsmen like Diego Maradona and Mike Tyson; these are not people who are mediocre – they were on top of the world. They were blessed with natural talent that God gave them, but when people forget God and put their faith in other things, like money or drink or drugs, their success will evaporate and their good names will be tarnished.

From what I have said and the examples I have given, it is obvious that it is mostly players from abroad, or from different ethnic backgrounds in Britain, who feel the most comfortable with declaring their religious beliefs. There are obvious reasons. As more money came to be invested in football and clubs began to compete at the highest level, British clubs imported players from all over the world. These players have brought their own cultures and their own national characteristics with them. Those of us who are from African and Caribbean countries tend to be less inhibited about showing our feelings, and especially our religious feelings; it is in our nature and our upbringing to rely on God for everything in our lives. In Britain, when you are out of work or living in poverty, you will be given a reasonable amount on which to live, and there is social housing. In countries such as Trinidad and Tobago, people don't depend on a welfare state, because there isn't one really. When you do not have, you do not automatically get. You cannot turn to the government when you need help. That teaches you, when you are in poverty and need, to pray for divine intervention and to depend on God for help.

Many black players have been brought up by their families to call on the name of the Lord in times of trouble and need. It isn't just those who have been raised in the Caribbean or Africa; there are black British players who have the same religious culture. In the past, it was a struggle for black players to get established, and, because of their background, the only help they had was the Almighty. God opened the door for them, and they are now telling people, 'This is what God has done for me in my chosen profession, and he can do the same for you in your life.'

I have learnt about Scotland and studied the story of John Knox, a man of God who preached almost 500 years ago that Scotland would be saved and become a blessed nation, the 'Land of the Book'. Scottish missionaries went to Africa and around the world to places such as the Caribbean to preach the Gospel. Now it is being reversed, because people from Africa and the Caribbean are bringing their faith back to Britain.

You look around and you do not see many people in

Britain proclaiming their faith and speaking about God; look in the churches and half of them are near empty. The people do not have time for God any more; they just want to get on with their lives, but they know something is missing. What is missing is God and the meaning and love he brings to our lives.

Football is considered a macho sport, and people might think you are soft or whatever for being a Christian, and maybe they're going to be critical of you for that. So you have got to be strong and say, 'No, this is what I believe.' Sometimes it makes you more of a man to stand up and say that you do believe in Jesus Christ than to hide it. Of course, it is still a very small percentage of players who are prepared publicly to declare their faith. I am sure there are many more believers in the game, but they prefer to keep it to themselves – that is their personal choice, and I would never criticise them for that. But when it comes to the things that are God's, I would never be ashamed or afraid to speak up. It is my way of life, and the Lord Jesus Christ told us to go into the world and preach the Good News.

I am happy and proud to say with Gavin Peacock and the other members of 'God's XI': I am a Christian first and a footballer second.

Chapter Nine

I'M A BELIEVER

Whenever I scored at Ibrox, they would play the old Monkees hit 'I'm A Believer', and when we needed encouragement, the Rangers fans would wave the 'Keep Believing' banner. I smiled when I saw headlines like 'Halo, Halo' instead of the old sectarian chant 'Hello, Hello' or 'Marvin Puts Rangers on the Road to Salvation'. That was just newspaper fun, but it was also getting over the message about belief, and it showed that even playing football can be a testimony.

It was the same when I put 'God bless' on every autograph. People weren't used to that, but eventually, if I didn't put it, they would give the autograph back to me so that I could add it.

Football makes it much easier to proclaim the Gospel. The game has a worldwide influence – there is not a country in the world where they do not play football of some kind, even if it has to be with an improvised ball. Footballers therefore have an opportunity to be an influence for good in the world. Prominence in the game gives status, because people will listen to what players from clubs such as Rangers and Celtic have to say on any subject.

Whether I do it in so many words or by example, I

know young people in particular are prepared to listen attentively to what I have to say. When I am around, people are talking religion as well as football. Years ago, you couldn't get a player going to a big club and mentioning God. It was not acceptable, and many players didn't have time for religion. I just let them know that Jesus Christ would help the team – and God kept backing up my word with actions.

When people all around the club and the ground started saying 'God bless, Marvin', it showed me there was a higher purpose in me being at such a high-profile institution, where religion of a kind was talked about but God was never really mentioned. I felt I had managed to be a blessing to Rangers with my footballing ability but also that God had used me, because I know they will never forget to 'Keep Believing'.

That slogan is forever associated with that amazing day when we won the championship. And when my faith allowed me to come back from serious injury, it also made people think. I know that, although they won't all come out openly, God has touched people at that club one way or another.

I can see that, apart from the success on the football field, or maybe because of it, there is a sense of mission about my being here in Scotland. In making the transition at that particular point in time, I was answering a calling. Since then, through football and becoming well known, the Lord Jesus Christ has spoken through me in the interviews I've given to the media and in everything I've done. As far as I can see, God has known that this nation would be turning away from him sooner or later. Despite knowing the Gospel, too many Scots these days have been making a U-turn away from Christ. I really believe I was brought to Scotland to testify. God ordained me as a pastor in Scotland. I'm still on a journey here, and I don't know where or how it will end; I don't know what the full picture is – I'm only human! I'll wait and see what is the will of God for Marvin Andrews.

The physical things matter, but belief is even more important. When any famous player is interviewed – David Beckham or Thierry Henry or whoever – and you always hear them say, 'I always believed from when I was young that one day I was going to be doing this,' they all use that word 'belief'. I happen to believe God when He says, 'All things are possible to him who believes'. It is as simple as that. The word of God does not lie.

Non-believers have tried to turn my religion into a caricature, but they cannot make fun of God. As a Christian, I know you are going to go through persecution and people are going to try to make a joke of it. These are things I have been through. But I also know that, without my church, I am a dead man walking.

Many were scornful when I turned down the move to Dundee United after praying to the Lord and then later went to Rangers. I never questioned either decision, because they were made for me; everything that has happened in my life has turned out to have a reason. Sometimes I've had to pinch myself to believe that I was playing for such a great club in Scotland and Europe, but it was also a testimony to what God can do for you if you have that faith and trust.

I have never stood up in the dressing-room and said, 'Come on, boys, start believing in God.' I believe in the power of example, and I am not here to force my beliefs on anybody. Just by my actions, I hope to let people know that God is real and alive and can help. I was happy to respond when players like Dado Prso and Fernando Ricksen asked me serious questions and were prepared to have a conversation about religion, and some of the young guys said they admired me for my beliefs. They might not have come out and said they were churchgoers; they might have been shy or afraid their mates would slag them off, but it showed that I had somehow touched them in their hearts or put the seed there.

Barry Ferguson said on my DVD *With God Nothing Is Impossible* that he could sit down with me and listen to me. Barry, captain of Rangers and Scotland, is a very high-profile player, and for a man of such stature to say that means a great deal to me. It shows that I have affected his life in some way through my belief.

Sometimes, fellow Rangers players would come up to me and ask 'Will God help us?' That happened frequently when we were five points behind Celtic in the title race with just a couple of games to go and everyone was very nervous that the championship might slip away from us. I would say, 'Yes, He will help. Just believe and you'll see.'

I said it in the newspapers, and people asked 'Is Marvin crazy?' But the way we won the championship after an amazing sequence of events proved the power of faith to me – and to others.

Sometimes, teammates have asked me to say a prayer for them and the team. Maybe they meant it half-humorously, but I have always done it because I, for one, totally believe in the power of prayer. The boys might have made jokes about it and asked me what God was saying, but at least they were asking about Him. They knew my trust was in God, and they respected that.

I'M A BELIEVER

During tight games, I would be praying to myself for God to be on our side, that He might do a miracle and give us a goal or something else that would be beneficial to the team. Of course, we lost games, but it didn't weaken my belief. Some things happen in life because they are meant to make you stronger and wiser or make you grow.

I have been asked about my reaction when an opponent fouls me or 'goes over the top' in a tackle on me. My answer has always been the same: I will not retaliate because I know that is what the Devil wants me to do, to put me to shame. People would say, 'Oh, he's a Christian and yet he's retaliating instead of turning the other cheek.' With God's help, I will never get sent off for retaliating or arguing with the referee.

The power of faith to heal the body has been proven through me. I believe God can work through conventional medicine. As I have said, I am not scared of doctors or surgery, and if God told me to undergo surgery, I would be the first person on the operating table – but I pray, believing that God will heal me. No doctor created Marvin Andrews; God is the one who created me. Doctors do fantastic work, for which they have studied and trained, and I respect that, but there are certain things that doctors cannot do that God can.

When I was told that I would need an operation and then six weeks' recuperation, I did not dismiss the specialist's opinion, and I am most certainly not telling people who are injured to ignore the doctors. But I prayed to God, believed what He was telling me, took the physiotherapy and went out and played without any further pain or harm. Of course, the doubt and fear were there within me. The Devil brings that fear, and it is always there. But my faith was stronger than it. Doubts came, and all different kinds of people were speaking negatively. It was a very hard time for me; that was why I had to keep on constantly reading the Bible, constantly praying. God kept telling me 'Keep believing, keep trusting', and that gave me strength.

I sincerely believe I overcame my injuries through prayer and spiritual healing. When you are a patient going to a doctor, why do you go? Because you believe he can help. You never go to somebody who can't help you, and it is the same with God. You pray because you want an answer. That doesn't mean a big voice in your ears; it can be a still, small voice, through your spirit or through the Bible. God can speak to you through a billboard on the wall, but don't expect him to speak unless you speak to him first through prayer.

Being a Christian is also about the way that you live. The bottom line is that you live a cleaner life – you don't go about swearing or having sex with people you don't know or love and are not married to. I was not living a righteous life before, and that is why I wanted to become a born-again Christian when I came to the church in Kirkcaldy. I never really did anything wrong before, but I was living the life of the world and did some crazy things: being with girls, drinking and gambling. I wasn't a betting addict or anything like that, but I used to do it for fun, and now I don't. I don't drink much or get drunk. If I have a drink, I'll make it a soft drink, although I don't see anything wrong with a pint of beer or a glass of wine. I just don't see the sense in being like those people who go out to get drunk and end up falling over.

Anywhere I go now, religion comes up in conversation. I might be in a nightclub with my friends, drinking my fresh orange and lemonade, watching things and enjoying the social atmosphere. People come up to me and tell me they used to go to church and talk about the problems they were having, although they had never told anyone else before. God has given me the wisdom to speak to them wherever and whenever I meet them and perhaps be able to change their lives forever. That is not meant in an arrogant way, because I do not have that power within myself. I want to be obedient and humble and let God change people's lives.

Even on the football field, with all that is going on and all that you hear around you, I refrain from swearing because I know God is in control of me. If a foul goes against me, I don't go up to the referee and start shouting; I use my Christian self-control and try to avoid getting a yellow card.

Yes, I have been sent off for a bad challenge, but I would never go out with the intention of hurting somebody. There was one occasion when I was forced to defend my style of play because there had been a lot of talk about what was called my 'no-holds-barred approach' and a player had ended up in hospital.

In a Livingston game against Kilmarnock, their keeper, Gordon Marshall, and I went up for the ball from a cross into his goalmouth and I felt something hit my head. At first, I thought it was his elbow, but then I saw him go down and it turned out to have been a sickening clash of our heads. I was left with a sore head, but Gordon was stretchered off with blood pouring from a head wound and spent the next two nights in hospital. It was very worrying, and I prayed hard, but every time you go up in the goalmouth it can be a dangerous situation.

These things happen in football, just as I know there

are feuds and paying off scores – especially when a teammate has been badly injured by a deliberate foul. I just think that a football player is trying to earn a living, to feed his family, his brothers and sisters, and make a better life. That is why I could never go in with the intention of perhaps breaking that person's leg, or his nose, or damaging his sight. If anyone wanted to do that to me because of the way I have played, that is their business. I know God protects me and will not allow me to be seriously harmed. Mind you, I will always protect myself too. I am not just going to lie down and say, 'Kick me now.'

The fame that football brings means you are constantly in the media and whatever you say can go everywhere; first of all, it is published to tens of thousands, then it can be published to millions all over the world through the Internet. When doing interviews, I ask God for the wisdom to answer every question brought before me in the right way, because anyone reading these interviews can be touched by God. They are not my words; they will be coming from me, but it is the will of God. However, there was one occasion when I was pilloried as a result of an interview I *didn't* give.

In February 2006, it was reported that in a newspaper interview I had labelled homosexuals as 'an abomination' and offered to 'cure' a Scottish politician who is a lesbian. In fact, I did not do the interview. What happened was that Pastor Joe spoke to a journalist for over an hour, which included saying that what homosexuals are doing is against the will of God. I met the journalist for five minutes on the stairs as he was leaving and he asked me if I agreed with what Pastor Joe had said. I said it was all in the Bible, and that became the front-page story. The editors must have asked themselves whose comment would sell papers – Pastor Joe's, who is known only to his flock, or the Rangers player's? Unknown to either Pastor Joe or myself, the story coincided with the gay marriage of a female MSP, so the headline became 'Marvin Andrews condemns MSP'.

I had never even heard about the marriage, and neither of us had mentioned it, yet it was being said that 'Marvin Andrews hates gays', or 'Marvin Andrews says gays are going to Hell'. They wanted to create a conflict between us and gays to make a better story.

For the record, let me state my position clearly. I do not hate gay people; they are human beings just like me. What I am saying is that what they are doing is against the will of God – not against me, but against God. I am here to tell them so, because if I do not tell them, God will hold me responsible for not telling them. If they still want to do it, that's well and good for them. There will be a judgement, and it is not Marvin Andrews' judgement. I have no problem meeting and talking to someone who is gay. There are people who have come to the church saying they are gay, but their spirit has changed and they have gone on to get married to a member of the opposite sex. In our church, we have experience of people we know who have been in that position.

We are not here to condemn someone who is homosexual; all we are saying is that God will help them to overcome that desire, which is ungodly. We are simply quoting what the Bible says. The Book of Genesis says that God destroyed the city of Sodom because 'their sin was so grievous', and in the New Testament the Book of Jude says that it was punishment for 'going after strange flesh', which is accepted to mean homosexuality.

I am not going to contradict my beliefs. I don't care if 100,000 people are against me; I'll stand on the word of God. I have been portrayed as hating these people. I don't, but when I talk to them I have to let them know that I believe what they are doing is wrong. I am not forcing my beliefs about homosexuality on anybody. It is up to them to listen or to disregard it, and I am not going to hate them for what they decide to do.

My family, the island of Trinidad and the whole of the Caribbean are all very religious. There are a lot of churches, and people don't go anywhere without praying every morning and night. That is how Caribbean people live, because they believe that without God there is no hope for them. Not everyone in the T&T national team is a Christian, but we all pray together before games, because everyone is brought up that way.

For the same reason, the Zion Praise Centre is so important to me. We sing praises unto God and the minister preaches from the Bible to give us more wisdom and understanding. I find it helps me to react in the right way to all kinds of situations. It is not like other churches, where you just stand up, sing hymns and listen to prayers and readings and sermons. It is like gospel music, and we are all singing, dancing and clapping, and people are playing instruments such as tambourines and drums. It's a time of happiness and rejoicing, which is fun and gives you a great feeling.

When I had a Sunday game, if it was at all possible, I would get to the morning service. Even if it might mean as little as a quick ten minutes of sermon at an eleven o'clock service or a snatched couple of verses of a hymn, I was showing my respect and gratitude to the Lord – and it put me in the right frame of mind for the test that was coming in that afternoon's match.

Our church is a prayer centre, more like a clinic or a health centre than your traditional churches. Every day, people come from different areas, some from right across Scotland, with different problems – physical, emotional or financial – and we pray with them for God's help.

In Scotland, people have turned away from God and the Bible. It could not be called the 'land of the Book' today. Sunday church attendances are dwindling, so are baptisms and marriages, and while many pay lip-service to religion, for the vast majority it does not show in the way they live their lives. There is still Christian life, and many would say they live by Christian values, but the beliefs and the faith of the people are not as strong as they once were. We have to pray for the nation that it will return to true belief in God.

Football has replaced religion for many people. They will put their hands in the air and sing and actually worship the successful manager and the players. But put the same people in church and you get silence.

Through the church, I have been privileged to see what faith can achieve – even in the darkest days and through the worst things that can happen in people's lives. The greatest example of how belief can overcome the worst of tragedies is a lady called Jackie Oswald. Jackie lost her thirty-eight-year-old husband Andrew and her children Nathan (four), Jemma (three) and two-year-old twins Charlotte and Charlene when fire swept through their house in the Fife village of Steelend. She escaped by jumping out of a first-floor window. Her only surviving daughter, Suzanne, who was six, was at primary school when the fire broke out. A lady who came to our church knew her, and Pastor Joe went to see her. She started coming to church, and when Pastor Joe was away, I was preaching and took the opportunity to talk to her.

I prayed and told her that she could make it through this terrible time, that God could still turn her life around. The same God who had given her those children would see that every one of them went to heaven. She came with her remaining daughter, and, although she had been through so much, she gradually got stronger in her belief and trust in God. Jackie was eventually baptised at a service at the local swimming pool. As a deacon, I went along and gave her weekly Bible class, and little Suzanne came to our Sunday school.

Giving her life to Christ gave her a peace that no one else could give her. She refused an offer of bereavement counselling and said that coming to church had given her the answer. Gradually, she managed to handle her grief and come to terms with her loss, except perhaps at birthdays. God restored her life, and she got back peace and joy, and it is all happening for her again.

People find it hard to explain how something so terrible can happen, but the Bible says in John 10:10 that, 'The thief does not come except to steal, and to kill, and to destroy.' The ultimate thief described by Jesus, the murderer and destroyer lying behind all of the world's tragedies, is the Devil. God gave Jackie her husband and those children, and God would not have taken them away in that horrible fashion. It was the Devil who took them away and tried to destroy her life.

Jackie was in the pit of despair – who would not be? – and, of course, she will always feel that loss; but God has restored her life and given her a new family.

Many people do not believe that the Devil exists – that

is his greatest trick – but you only have to look at the newspapers and see what is happening at home and around the world to see the evidence that he is alive and very, very real.

In September 2006, I was ordained a pastor of the Zion Praise Centre and can now conduct weddings and communion services. Football has helped me in my ministry, as people come to the church because of my fame. It is because of the confidence that I have built on the football field that I am able to stand before congregations, lead them, answer questions and offer them spiritual guidance. One observer who came to watch me pointed out that when I get going, a sermon can last as long as a football match! More seriously, he wrote, 'It is evident that this is not a sportsman who has "got religion". Religion has got him, and his faith shapes every step he takes.'

To keep our church going when Pastor Joe was away, visiting other churches and congregations around the world, I started preaching the Word of God to the people. Now that I have been ordained, I will preach even when he is here and the spirit moves us. I prepare by praying and asking God for the words he wants me to speak. He will tell me what subject to talk about, and the actual words are not mine, because I believe they are put there in my mind and I only have to open my heart and my mouth and the right words will come out. It has often happened that, afterwards, someone in the congregation has come forward and said, 'That word was just for me.' It touches me so much when I realise how God operates. God has put that specific word into my mouth, and if it speaks to one person, I have done what God wanted me to do. Nothing that I speak from that pulpit is my own. It is the result of prayer and asking for the specific message that the Lord needs me to give on that particular day at that particular service.

All ministers are different, and some will want to spend time writing a long sermon and getting it exactly right. There is nothing wrong with that, but I'm not like ministers or priests who sit in their studies, writing their sermons, looking up the right Scriptures to quote and polishing the phrases. I am fortunate that I don't have to spend a whole day getting a sermon ready!

I know, because it has happened to me, that the Word God gives you is so powerful that you can meditate on it for a long period of time. And, because I have studied my Bible and memorised it, God gives me the specific Scriptures to use and the actual message for the particular occasion. I may not realise it, but there may be someone in the congregation with their own special problem and God wants to pass on the answer.

The BBC *Football Focus* programme on footballers and their faith that I've already talked about showed me preaching about the evils of drugs and drink, but it was really a sermon on trust. It goes like this:

'We are living in a world where people put their trust in material things, things they can see and touch and own – like their house, land, car, bank account or their job. You can even put your trust in your family or your best friend, and at the end of the day you can get let down in some way. You see it in marriage, where a husband or wife tells their marriage partner "I love you so much" and "I'll do anything for you" but, before you know it, they have betrayed that husband or wife.

'God says, "Cursed is the man or woman who puts trust in Man"; meaning that if you put all your trust in a human, you are going to be disappointed. The Lord says, "Blessed is the man or woman who puts trust in God."

'God wants you to put Him first and human beings after Him. We are all human and imperfect, we all make mistakes and God is trying to warn us about putting all our trust in human frailty.

'Drugs and alcohol are killing the nation and world, and getting people to put their trust in these things is the Devil's work. When they take them, they feel good for five or ten minutes, but God can give a great feeling of peace and joy and happiness with no evil effects. Drink or drugs can give a boost or a hyper, but it is only temporary and the consequences can be long-lasting and disastrous for the person and for society.

'That is why the Bible says, "The blessing of God leads to riches and no sorrow." If God does not bless a thing, there will be sorrow added to it – and the proof is in the way people live their lives and the things they use which cause so much unhappiness in the world.'

A sermon like that goes down well with the congregation because all I am doing is just preaching the Word as I receive it. Nothing that I speak from the pulpit is of my own knowledge or understanding; everything that I speak, I can show you in the Bible, being spoken by a man of God or by Jesus Christ himself.

For most of my life, I could not have done anything like that. When my mate Tony Rougier first took me to the Zion Praise Centre in Kirkcaldy, even though I was becoming a well-known footballer performing in front of thousands of people, I was one of the most terrified individuals ever. I was so shy and reluctant that even to set foot inside the church took an effort. I was so self-conscious that I felt embarrassed to stand among the congregation, to sing and clap my hands.

As a young boy growing up, I had always been to the Catholic Church, whose style of worship is quite reserved, and – even in a happy and outgoing land like Trinidad – the congregation did not express themselves as we do in our Pentecostal services in the Zion Praise Centre. That does not make us any better than them or mean that their faith is not as fervent as ours; it just means that people see God differently and worship Him differently.

As I have said, I eventually saw some things that I did not like about the Catholic Church, and I stopped attending at the age of 13, when my grandmother died. Between then and the age of 22 I did not go to a service. I still prayed and read the Bible, though, but without guidance. Nobody taught me about the Bible, and I used to read it not knowing the meaning and the power of what I was actually reading. Although I was young, it was a decision I made all on my own – and, given the way my life and my faith have turned out, good things came of it.

When Pastor Joe told me some time later that he wanted me to preach, I was astonished. To talk in front of all these people, to know what to say and to be able to convince them, seemed beyond me, and I actually felt worry and fear. At first, I would sweat with apprehension about standing in the pulpit. People are puzzled about that because they think that playing before thousands of people on big occasions in national stadiums must have given me confidence. I have to laugh, because there is no comparison. As a footballer, I know I have been blessed with talent, I can rely on my skills and I have been given a job to do as a member of a team. Playing football is something that I love, and I just have to perform as a defender, react to what is happening around me and express myself in a natural way. In the pulpit, I have a heavy responsibility to say something that is important and that means something to every single person who is listening to my words. I have to pray that I do not say something that comes out in the wrong way or is not what God wants me to say. Everybody in the congregation is watching you and listening intently to what you are saying. There will be people sitting in that congregation who need help. By the words that I speak, with God's help, it might change their lives forever. They may become somebody they never believed they could become because of the Word that has been put into my heart.

As I grew in faith and kept praying, I was given more confidence, more trust in the Spirit, more wisdom and more knowledge. Before I knew it, preaching in front of a congregation was nothing to me. I have got to the point where I go to different churches and congregations all over the land, speaking to grown-ups, youth groups and young kids. I have to say that to speak to the young is harder than speaking to adults. You have to say something in their own language, in a way they understand, about the things they know and experience in their own lives.

My religion is based firmly on the Bible, and I find its best expression in the Pentecostal Church, whose people believe in the Holy Spirit. In Acts you read Paul telling us that Jesus said, 'Before I go, I will pray to the Father to send you a comforter which is the Holy Spirit.' In Acts Chapter 1, you read that on the day of Pentecost, the Holy Spirit came down and people were speaking in tongues. Some churches do not believe in the Holy Spirit, but being Pentecostal Christians means we believe in and do everything the Bible says. It does not make us perfect or better than any other believer, but we follow what Christ said: the work that He has done, we shall do as well. When the Holy Spirit comes upon you, you have the power. That's why we can tell people that when we pray to God, God speaks.

We take praise very seriously, and ours is an active and joyful form of worship. We come before His presence singing, playing instruments, beating drums – whatever it takes. After all, the Bible says, 'Make a joyful noise unto the Lord.' In the Old Testament, the Psalms show us that David was a man of praise – every opportunity he got, he praised God. In the Old Testament days, dance was one of the most important forms of worship. Just talking about it gets the Spirit moving in me and I start snapping my fingers . . .

When you worship in that way, people are moved, they receive healing and get wisdom. Other people prefer to take their worship more casually. I've even seen people with their hands in their pockets while they are supposed to be worshipping God. To me, that is disrespectful to God. There is no way I could go in front of the Prime Minister or the Queen or the Royal Family with my hands in my pockets, so why would you do it to the Creator of heaven and earth, the person who has your life in His hands?

I have seen hero-worship in football, and, let's face it, I've received some of that myself. Every human being loves to receive praise and be worshipped. If someone talks highly about you, you may try to seem modest, but something stirs inside you and you feel good. You would do anything to help that person when they are needy, because they have praised you and spoken well of you. It is the same thing with God. He loves you to praise and honour Him, because the Bible says, 'Let everything that hath the breath of life in it give me praise.' I believe that even the trees praise God. People may say that is crazy, but trees are alive and not dead. If you listen, when the breeze blows, the trees stir, make a sound, and that is one way of nature giving God praise.

It has been said to me that singing and dancing in church is not natural for British people because their national character is that they are cool and do not like to show emotion. Yet they will let themselves go for the traditional things they are used to. At a football game, you hear people shouting and singing to their team until they are hoarse. Rangers and Celtic have their songs, Liverpool fans sing 'You'll Never Walk Alone' and even Raith Rovers fans sing the 'Geordie Munro' song, 'I'd rather stay here in Kirkcaldy'. Even if it is freezing, football supporters will rip their tops off in exultation and wave them over their heads. Believe me, when you are on the field and hear sixty to a hundred thousand people cheering, shouting and singing, you cannot help being stirred by it. They are carried away by their enthusiasm, fervour and belief. Call it whatever you want, but they are giving praise to their team.

You get the same kind of thing at pop and folk concerts, at the Last Night of the Proms and at anything that brings people together and inspires them. So why can that not be transposed to the church, where there is even more reason to be moved? Why do worshippers feel that when they set foot inside a church, they have to become calm, quiet and reserved, not pray too hard or sing too loud?

I can understand that they are showing respect, but we believe worship is a celebration. When you're alone in the shower, you sing your heart out. When you go to a party, you will sing, laugh, dance and enjoy yourself – and you don't need a drink to show your happiness. We believe that going to the House of God can be like a party and we can praise, sing and dance as the spirit leads us.

There is a time and place for everything, so God is not against people going to a football match and getting involved, or against people going to a party and enjoying themselves with their friends. But when it is time to come to God, don't come into the house of God and play at being the holiest person, the best angel; as the Bible says, 'Enter His house, His gates, with thanksgiving; enter His courts with praise.'

Being brought up in the Catholic Church, I know the importance to them of ritual, dress and system. Their form of worship is laid down and has to be done precisely in a certain way each time. There is nothing wrong in dressing up in your finest clothes and looking good for God. But that should not mean someone who cannot afford nice clothes, and does not have a suit or a Sunday dress, cannot come to church. That is where formality becomes a problem, because the Bible says, 'Render your heart, not your garments.'

Some people going to church do the opposite: they render their fine garments while their heart is unclean. It is what is in their heart that counts. Some people go to church to be seen doing the proper thing and to look good, but their real intention is not to worship God. Other people come in shabby clothes because that is all they have. They still come into church, because their intention is simply to praise God, and they should never be made to feel uncomfortable because of their outward appearance. They may come just in jeans and a T-shirt, but in their heart they are giving God all they have. I will dress up for special occasions and for preaching, but I often worship in T-shirt, training trousers and trainers or sandals.

'Faith healing' is a part of our faith that fascinates people. Personally, I cannot understand why that should be, because it has been practised in churches from Biblical times. It made the headlines when I refused surgery and my injuries were healed by prayer – especially the cruciate ligament damage when I was at Rangers. I do not really like the term 'faith healing'; this is simply believing in God's power. You could have faith in all sorts of inanimate things – totems, images, man-made objects – to heal you, but that does not mean these things will make you well. You can have faith in a physician to heal you, and when the doctor's treatment works, you could call that faith healing. In Mark 16, when Jesus appeared to his disciples, he said, 'Lay hands upon the sick and they shall recover.'

I do not claim to have supernatural power; I am not a magician or someone special. All we do is pray to the Almighty God on behalf of that man or woman with whatever sickness, disease or problem he or she is going through and ask that He will transform that person's situation. There is no drug or potion, no trick or scheme; there is nothing physical. It is all about believing that the words of Jesus Christ mean what they say and, by the laying on of hands, our faith will make the sick person recover. The person also has to believe in God. I have faith that God can touch that person, but if that person does not believe, God will not touch them.

You could go to the Prime Minister, knowing he has the power to make things happen, but you know the limits of that power and you know that such power can be taken from him, so you do not expect a miracle. When you go to God, you have to believe that He exists and that He has the power to heal the sick, blind, deaf and crippled, and that He has the power to raise the dead.

I know there are preachers who perform healing and raise money through it, but, for me, this is not something that you can make a job out of. I have seen a man on TV who claims that the spirit of the Apostle Paul comes into him, so he goes about healing people who are suffering from bad backs, sore necks and stress problems, and takes money for the 'cure'. Nowhere in the Bible do you read of Jesus healing the sick and saying 'OK, that will be twenty quid, please!'

If you have a piece of equipment that fails, you take it to the manufacturers, because they made it and they know how it works. So why should God, who made man from dust, not have the answer to all human problems? He made my head, heart, lungs, liver and every part of me – including that famous cruciate ligament! So why do people think he cannot repair my body?

Linvoy Primus had the same experience as me. He suffered a bad knee injury, refused to have an operation and is still playing top-class football. Like me, he put his faith in God to heal him, and He did. There was one difference: Linvoy said he felt something like 'electricity' in his knee. It can happen, and, because he believed, he could feel the power of God working in him. I have known people who said they could immediately feel the same power working in the part of the body that was damaged or diseased, while others are healed over a period of time. Linvoy felt that God was touching him, and he could feel something was happening within his knee. This is the miraculous power of God.

It is like the story in the New Testament about the woman with the issue of blood. The moment she touched the hem of Jesus Christ's garment, she felt she was free from that infirmity. So what Linvoy was feeling had already been recorded in the Bible happening to other people.

The healing of my injuries occurred more slowly, but just as surely. The Bible says, 'As your faith, let it be done unto you', and God tests your faith to see how much you believe.

You may have noticed that I seem to have a biblical quotation to back up everything I say. I read the Bible constantly, and, in spite of years of study, I am learning every day. There are many things that still have to be revealed to me, and that can only happen through reading the Bible. Besides my reading, I hear Pastor Joe and others making references, and I search them out with a highlighting pen. My own copy of the Bible is multicoloured, because on so many pages there are verses I have highlighted for study. That is the good thing I have found about the Bible: you just cannot get enough of it. You can never say, 'Now, I know it all.' To this day, I am still learning and will go on learning to the end of my days.

The Bible is not like a story-book that you can read and know everything in its pages; no matter how much you read it, you cannot know all of God. You may read a verse in the Good Book ten times and God can give you a different revelation of it ten times, depending on the circumstances, on what is happening in the world and in your life when you're reading it. When you are up, when you are down or when you are not feeling well, there is a special word for you.

The Bible is a manual, and God wants you to use it constantly, renewing your mind daily. In the worst of Scottish weather, I have felt blue, and the Bible told me, 'This is the day that the Lord has made. I will rejoice and be glad in it.' For someone like me, coming from a warmer climate, that is a strong statement! It might be snowing or stormy, it might be minus one outside, but because it is the day the Lord has made, you can rejoice because you are alive and you are blessed to be part of it.

Footballers make a lot of money, and they are quite right to enjoy it while they can – because, although the career can be very high-earning, it can also be short-lived. The sport has given me financial stability and the power to help and be a blessing to other people's lives. I don't have all that many possessions, but I am not against them. God wants us to prosper and enjoy life to the fullest. There is nothing wrong with having a fancy house, a nice car, living in luxury, and if I don't have money, I cannot help a poorer person. But there has to be something more. These things mustn't be your main focus, and you can't worship them.

I am happy that I can help to support my auntie, who brought me up, and my dad and mum and other members of my family. And it gives me pleasure that for years there have been kids in Trinidad playing their street football in Raith Rovers, Livingston and Rangers kits.

To me, family and marriage are very important things, but I watch people and I have seen some who have been

I'M A BELIEVER

taken right down in their lives by problems in their marriages. Some day, I will be directed to the right wife and have the right family. I am not the sort of guy to say 'I love you' and a couple of years down the line run into problems and break up. It is important for me not to rush in but to wait for the person whom God has destined for me as a help-mate.

You must never be in the position where you are prepared to do anything, say anything or hurt anyone to become rich and famous. Money and possessions can be a blessing, but without God it is just an empty life, no matter how wealthy you become. I have a comfortable lifestyle, but I try to keep it simple and humble. The one thing I try to refrain from is misguided pride. Too many people who become wealthy forget where they came from and struggle to know their real place in life. I'm well known, but if there's a queue, I'll take my place at the back and wait my turn, because I am no better a person than anybody else.

I've gone to some bad neighbourhoods and been asked 'What's a football star like you doing in this place?' I hate that, because it implies that, since I've made a name for myself, they class me as 'something' and themselves as nothing. I feel blessed that I can go into such places and tell them that they can become something, not solely in football but in anything they choose. The one thing I feel I can be really proud of is my achievement in life and in football – but, as I keep testifying, I owe it all to God.

Chapter Ten

THE ROVER RETURNS

When I left Rangers, there was interest from English Premiership and Championship clubs, with talk of seven-figure deals. SPL clubs were also making enquiries. So there was a great deal of shock and bafflement when I ended up back at my first club, Raith Rovers, playing in the Scottish Second Division.

I must say there cannot have been many football signing negotiations which have been brokered by a government leader and world statesman, as well as a pastor of God!

Straight away, I would like to clear up one thing, without meaning any disrespect to Mr Gordon Brown. It was said that Gordon Brown, who is the local MP and a lifelong Raith fan who sold programmes at the ground as a boy, had made me an offer I couldn't refuse. I just want to say there is someone even more important than Mr Brown . . .

When I was freed by the new Rangers management, it took almost two months' praying and asking God for directions to confirm my next move. Agents were even calling the church trying to contact me, but I was only looking for one source of guidance, and that was the Almighty God.

To be honest, I left Ibrox a bit disappointed as a human being. I had a great time at Rangers, but God told me I had fulfilled everything I was sent to Rangers to do and it was time to move on to the next chapter.

If it had been about what I wanted, I would probably have gone to the English Premiership, but now, deep down, when I pray, I have the peace and joy of having followed the will of God. For whatever reason, He wanted me in Kirkcaldy at that particular time, and I was just being obedient. If Manchester United had come in for me and God still wanted me in Kirckcaldy, I would not have gone. There were so many clubs interested in me from England and Scotland that I lost count. But my life is not moved by money; I am only moved by what God wants for me.

After I'd left in September 2000, Raith had gone through hard times, and there was a lot of unhappiness in the town and in Scottish football generally about the way the club was being run. Some very strange decisions were taken, and there was a bizarre period when Nicolas Anelka's agent brother, Claude, was appointed manager and brought in a number of his own footballers who were complete unknowns.

The club had dropped into the Second Division and was near bankrupt when a community buyout was arranged. This was greatly helped by the influence of Gordon Brown, who organised a group of local businessmen to fund the deal. I had continued to live in Kirkcaldy, my church is part of the community and I know how important it is to the town of Kirkcaldy to have a football team of which it can be proud.

I was very interested when approaches were made, through Gordon Brown, to see if I would go back to

Raith Rovers. Some people may think it strange that the Chancellor of the Exchequer would take time out from government business to arrange the transfer of a football player, but it shows his commitment as the local MP and his lifelong devotion to Raith Rovers.

I became even more intrigued when it was suggested it could mean more than just playing for Rovers; there would also be community involvement, working with young people – and, of course, it would mean I could stay close to the Zion Praise Centre in Kirkcaldy, where I was now a pastor.

Gordon Brown took the trouble to set up a meeting with myself and Pastor Joe at our church, and he came along himself with the club's new manager, Craig Levein. It was then that I realised how seriously they were treating the bid to get me back at Stark's Park. At the meeting, we discussed the project that clinched it for me, which was that the three-year deal would be in conjunction with the plan to set up the Marvin Andrews Youth Development Trust to do community work among young people in the area.

Craig Levein admitted that it was only after the meeting at the Zion Praise Centre that he believed I would sign. Announcing it to the media and the fans, he said, 'Marvin's willingness to buy into this project made the deal happen, and I am still shocked that we have pulled it off. Marvin is a deeply religious man, and this deal appealed to him not just in a football sense but in other areas of his life as well.

'The players were asking if Marvin was coming back, and, like me, they are all gobsmacked that he has actually signed. The club has ambitions, and a major part of this deal happening was Gordon Brown's input – I think his involvement showed Marvin and his people that we are deadly serious about what we are trying to achieve here.'

I am not interested in politics and have no intention of getting involved in them, but I know Gordon Brown as a very generous and honourable man. I also know he worked very hard and used all his influence, which is considerable, to make sure I returned to Raith. I was told he saw it as a symbol of the rebirth of the club from the mess into which it had slumped. My signing was part of a message that Gordon Brown, the directors and the town wanted to send out: that Raith Rovers were now a community club and were looking to the future, not just in terms of football success but also for the local people, especially the youngsters.

Gordon Brown's input was important because it made me see how, as a footballer, I could make a contribution which in other areas of my life is important to me. It also showed that, after all the problems, morale was being rebuilt and the club had ambitions.

Craig may have been 'gobsmacked' that I had signed, but there were so many special things about the deal that made it impossible for me to say 'no'. I owed Raith Rovers a lot for giving me my start in professional football, and the local people for making me feel at home in Kirkcaldy. It meant a lot to me when Craig told the fans, 'This club needs as much enthusiasm as it can get. It's been battered around a bit. Sometimes people walk around here with a little cloud on their head. We are trying to chase the clouds away.

'Marvin will give everyone a huge confidence boost, especially the young guys who will feed off his composure, and the fact he has turned down offers from England

and Scotland sends a great message to the fans. This is a club on the up.'

And then of course there was the Trust scheme that was being set up to help kids make something of their lives. Like youths everywhere, many of Kirkcaldy's younger generation were going astray and being destroyed through drugs or alcohol. Footballers are among the few people they look up to as role models, and I saw it as a good opportunity for me to help by at least getting them off the streets and away from idleness. Football alone won't help them, but they need someone to perhaps touch their lives, help them to realise the talent that God has blessed them with and let them realise their dreams and ambitions. Not everyone is a football fanatic; some like singing or dancing or expressing themselves in other ways, but my main concern is that they do not let their lives waste away.

So it was a big night for me on 2 March 2007 when a large group of teenagers between the ages of 13 and 18 turned up at Kirkcaldy High School's Community Facility for the first of our Friday night football sessions. Raith Rovers and Cowdenbeath Football Clubs gave their full support, including players and coaching staff. Showing how much of a community effort this project is, we are supported by youth workers from Fife Council's Community Services and funded by the Coalfields Regeneration Trust, Fife Council, the SFA and Sport Scotland. Mr David Somerville, Raith Rovers' chairman, summed it up when he said, 'This project is not about developing great footballers but providing these youngsters with something worthwhile to do when they would otherwise be hanging about the streets.'

When I saw the number of young people who had

turned up and how enthused they were, I really felt that I was giving something back to football and to the town that had adopted me.

But I must say that when I got back into training with Raith Rovers, it was down to earth with a bump! The first session under Craig Levein was in the local public park in an absolute downpour. We were up to our ankles in mud – a big difference from the luxurious Rangers training facility at Murray Park – but the spirit was great.

Everybody in football respected Craig as a player and now as a manager but most of all as a man of principle. It was because of his principles that he left his high-profile job as manager of Hearts, and Raith were lucky to get him, even for a short time, to help them through a difficult time.

However, we all knew he was at the club on a non-contract basis and it would only be a matter of time before a senior club in Scotland or England would approach him. It happened quicker than we thought, and, just a couple of weeks after I had signed, he became manager of Dundee United.

Again, Raith were fortunate to get a replacement manager of the calibre of John McGlynn, who is one of the most highly regarded coaches in the Scottish game and who had a solid record of achievement at Hearts. The players like him because he is a straight-talking man who also thinks deeply about the game and is ambitious for himself and his players. He told us his main aim is to get Rovers into the SPL. Of course, that is a long-term goal, but he believes that the club is very much a sleeping giant which, handled the right way, can climb into the top league.

After the troubles at Heart of Midlothian, where he was coach under Craig Levein, John decided that he wanted to be his own man and run a club the way he thought it should be run. He has one of the shrewdest brains in Scottish football, with very clear ideas about tactics, and, at first, it seemed that I did not fit into the system of play he wanted.

For his first few games, while he was sorting things out, I was on the bench, and questions were being asked about my absence from the team after all the ballyhoo about my signing. I was quite happy to train and be available for whenever the manager wanted me.

Although there was a big improvement in the team's performances, the wins just would not come, and Raith slipped down the table. The manager changed his preferred formation to make room for me at the heart of the defence, and suddenly we had a seven-game unbeaten run. More importantly, there were five victories in a row with no goals against us; I got on the scoring list and we were challenging for the play-offs and promotion back into the First Division.

John McGlynn said that he would not change a winning formula, and I was back where I wanted to be – doing my best for the club and the fans who are also my friends.

Chapter Eleven

GOD IS MY AGENT

I have never spent much time worrying about the future. That is in God's hands, and I leave those decisions to Him – even though they can sometimes cause a sensation.

People find it hard to contact me because I don't have an agent. God is my agent, and, for the moment, God wants me in Scotland, or at least in Britain, spreading the Gospel. If God spoke to me tomorrow and said, 'Marvin, I want you back in Trinidad,' I would be back in Trinidad. My life is not my own any more.

I can disobey God and be the unhappiest player in the world, but life is about happiness. I believe that if I go where God says I'm not supposed to be, only disaster and destruction can befall me. It is not for me to say if or when I will move on.

I do see myself trying to take my country back to the World Cup finals again. The qualifying cycle comes round so quickly, and I have been asked whether Raith Rovers, in the Scottish Second Division, is the best platform for me to do that. For me, it does not matter where I play. In Trinidad and Tobago, I played for a part-time brewery team and represented my country. It is all about the football you play and your own personal desire. Clubs don't motivate you; you have to motivate yourself and maintain your fitness and your personal standards.

My main purpose in life is to preach the Gospel. Football was the career I wanted for myself, but being a pastor of the church is a calling from God. I will just have to wait and see where that calling takes me.

The first aim of the Marvin Andrews Youth Development Trust is to get certain youngsters out of being idle by awakening their interest. It is true that Satan makes work for idle hands. I see young people after school or at weekends just hanging about, needing to be involved and looking for excitement. That is why they take drugs or drink alcohol, and before long they are doing things they cannot even remember.

My goal is to help these kids release the talent that is inside them. I know every one of them has been blessed with some special individual gift, and they just need help to bring it out so that in future they can be a benefit to their community and the wider world.

Our main objective is to show these youngsters that drink and drugs are not the best route to happiness. These things may give them a temporary high, but they must be made to realise that, using the talents God has given them, they can achieve real and longer-lasting happiness. We are starting off with football, but eventually I want to widen the scope. Boys have other interests besides football, and, although girls play football too and can be very good at it, more of them need to be involved as well. I see no reason why we cannot help young people of both sexes with things like acting, singing, being a beautician or whatever artistic interest they may have. We should be finding that special talent in each individual and igniting it, so that they can fulfil dreams and become something in life – just as I have been able to do through football.

People keep asking me whether I will go into coaching or managing, and I always answer that I really do not know. Rather than team tactics, which is not really my field, I prefer talking to young kids and letting them know that they can get a lot of achievement, satisfaction and fun out of football.

Football has taken me so far in a very short time. But I know that if it wasn't for God, there would have been no football career and no one would even have heard of Marvin Andrews.

The normal football career lasts ten or twenty years, working up through the levels of the game. All my football achievements have been over the last nine years, and the things I have achieved in that time seem to me to be supernatural. I remember those times in Trinidad where I had one pair of trainers, one pair of trousers, one T-shirt and played barefoot. Now, I have brought out a DVD and I can look at myself on it as captain of my country, qualifying for the World Cup. I am on video games, and youngsters come up to me and say, 'I've just been playing with you on PlayStation!'

I'm 31 now, and I see no reason why I cannot play for years yet. I just love playing football, because it is such an enjoyable game, and, God willing, it is my desire to go on and on. Even when I decide not to play at a professional level, I will want to play for fun. It has been an amazing life so far. Yet I believe God has been preparing me for something greater, whether it is inside or outside football.

My dream was to be a professional footballer and play at the highest level, and I have achieved that – but who knows how much higher I can go? As the slogan on my T-shirt says, 'With God . . .'